Microsoft SharePoint

For Beginners

A Comprehensive Step-By-Step Guide to Unlocking Peak Productivity and Collaboration with Microsoft SharePoint's Power Tools & Turbocharge Your Team's Performance

TABLE OF CONTENTS

CHAPTER 1
INTRODUCTION TO SHAREPOINT

Overview of SharePoint

What is SharePoint?

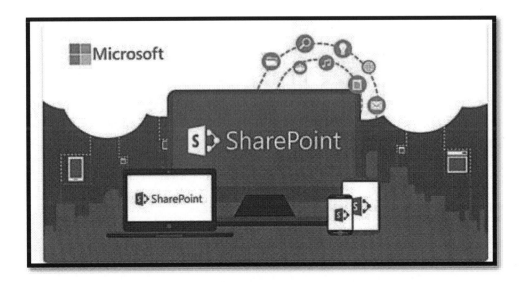

In today's changing business and collaborative world, businesses try to use technology to speed up operations, improve communication, and build a culture of creativity. SharePoint is a game-changing technology that has transformed how teams communicate, share information, and manage content. As we explore through the pages of this book, we will dig into the complex features of SharePoint, discovering its varied possibilities and demonstrating how it acts as a keystone in business collaboration. SharePoint has become an important tool for many types of joint business tasks since its launch in 2001. Microsoft SharePoint has gone through many versions over the years, with each one adding new features, making the user experience better, and improving speed. This change shows that Microsoft is always trying to meet the changing needs of people and companies. This book is a guide for both new and experienced SharePoint users, giving insights into the platform's design, core functions, and best practices for deployment. Whether you are an IT professional charged with managing SharePoint installations or a business user looking to take use of its collaborative capabilities, the material on these pages is designed to improve your knowledge and competency with this powerful platform. Furthermore, this book focuses on more than just technical topics. It focuses on the strategic use of SharePoint inside a company, stressing its role in increasing productivity, encouraging information exchange, and cultivating a collaborative culture. Real-world situations, case studies, and practical suggestions are interlaced throughout, providing readers with a comprehensive knowledge of SharePoint's use in a variety of corporate contexts.

SharePoint 2024 Key Features

SharePoint, built by Microsoft, goes beyond the typical bounds of a document management system. It is a complete web-based platform that allows companies to easily generate, organize, share, and retrieve information. SharePoint is meant to be a flexible solution, supporting varied business demands with its strong features and capabilities, ranging from document collaboration to process automation, intranet portals, and business intelligence integration.

Below are the features:

1. Create themes for SharePoint in Brand Centre
Get rid of the old, slow way of making and changing themes with the SharePoint Online Control Shell. Microsoft is giving you a better and new way to make themes right in the brand center. With a sleek and easy-to-use interface, you can now make and change themes in SharePoint. No more annoying code or dull graphics. This feature is being worked on right now, and it should be ready in June 2024. Get ready to make your SharePoint sites shine with your imagination!

2. Custom fonts for SharePoint
"How can we use our custom font in our intranet?" is one of the questions I get asked most often by clients. That's been the answer for too long (unless you want to break your site with an app customizer that doesn't work with Microsoft changes). Microsoft has finally listened to its users and begun working on this long-awaited tool that will also make your Viva Connections experience better. In March 2024, the roll-out is set to begin.

3. Section Backgrounds
You can now add your images to the section background of SharePoint Online pages and posts, which are a cool new feature that will make them, look better. The current option lets you pick from a small set of colors based on the site's style. This will give you more artistic freedom and flexibility. Microsoft will also offer settings that can be used to make the images easier to read and view. This tool should start to be available in February 2024.

4. Copilot for SharePoint
The fact that Copilot is coming to SharePoint is very exciting. Just by telling it what to do, AI can help you make your websites and pages. You can also have a chat with Copilot to make small changes to your site, like how it works and how it looks. Copilot is a type of license called "Copilot for Microsoft 365." In March 2024, Copilot for SharePoint should be out in the wild. Don't miss this chance to use Copilot to boost your creativity and productivity!

5. Pages Coauthoring
One of the best things about moving from on-premise to Microsoft 365 was being able to work on papers together in Teams and SharePoint. But we still had trouble when we tried to write news or SharePoint pages together. How often has someone else saved their version over yours and you lost the changes you made? Don't worry anymore! Coming soon is an update that will let people co-author SharePoint stories and pages. This means that you and your coworkers can work

at the same time on the same page in SharePoint without losing your changes. Thanks for this great feature. It will be very useful for sites with lots of information and writers. At this point, the update is set to come out in March 2024.

Document Management and Collaboration

SharePoint's Document Management and Collaboration are two interconnected parts of the platform that change how businesses handle information, encourage teamwork, and speed up their processes. Let's take a closer look at each of these areas to see how SharePoint works with document-based collaboration.

Document Management

- **Centralized archive**: SharePoint is a safe and well-organized place where teams can make, store, and handle a wide range of material. It acts as a central archive for documents. Users can easily get to the most recent versions of papers thanks to this storage, which gets rid of the mess of files that are spread out all over the place.
- **Version Control**: Version control is one of the most important features that keeps people from getting confused when they are working on the same text at the same time. Versioning in SharePoint keeps track of changes, so teams can go back to older versions if they need to. This makes sure that everyone is working with the most up-to-date information.
- **Metadata and Tagging**: SharePoint uses metadata and tagging to make it easy for businesses to organize and group documents. This method makes it easier to look for files and makes sure that users can quickly find specific files, even in large document stores.
- **Workflow Integration**: SharePoint works well with workflow automation, which speeds up processes that focus on documents. The platform has tools to simplify and improve many business processes, such as content review cycles and methods for document acceptance. This cuts down on the need for human work and boosts total efficiency.
- **Compliance and Security**: SharePoint has strong features like access limits, encryption, and audit logs because it knows how important security and compliance are. These steps not only keep private data safe but also make sure that companies follow the rules and laws in their business.

Collaboration

- **Real-Time Collaboration**: Teams can work together in real-time thanks to SharePoint's collaborative setting, which crosses regional borders. By letting users co-author papers and have talks within team sites, the platform creates a sense of community that is very important for modern businesses with teams that work in different places.
- **Team Sites and Portals**: SharePoint team sites give teams their places to work together. With document files, schedules, job lists, and statements, these sites can be changed to fit the needs of each team. SharePoint-based portals take this idea further by providing a single location for collaboration across the entire company.

- **Integration with Microsoft Teams**: The ability to work together better is increased by connecting SharePoint to Microsoft Teams, which is a Microsoft 365 collaboration tool. Teams use SharePoint as their main document storage system. This makes sure that all files shared and worked on by Teams members are easily handled through SharePoint.
- **Social Collaboration**: SharePoint has tools for social collaboration, such as user accounts, conversation boards, and news feeds. These things encourage people to share information, come up with new ideas, and feel like they belong in the group, which leads to a mindset of working together.
- **Custom Applications and Solutions**: SharePoint has tools that come out of the box, but it also has a strong structure for building applications. By letting companies make their apps and solutions that fit their specific collaboration needs, the platform's features can be expanded to fit different business processes.

Navigating SharePoint Sites and Libraries

Exploring the SharePoint Home Page

As soon as you log in to SharePoint, the start page is what you see. In the world of SharePoint, think of it as your customizable screen. As your main hub, it brings together all the important information you need and makes it easy to get to the tools and resources you use most often.

How to Access the Start Page

1. Signing in to SharePoint when you log in to SharePoint, you'll start off on the main page.
2. **Getting to SharePoint You can easily reach SharePoint from anywhere in Microsoft 365. Just use the app launcher:**
- Click on the app start button.
- Pick SharePoint from the options.

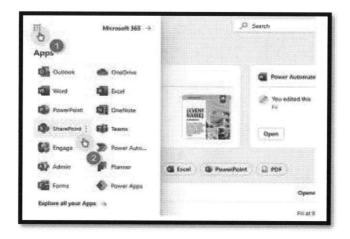

3. Through the house icon

- With one click, you can go straight to the start page from any SharePoint site or page.
- **Click on the link that looks like a house below the app menu icon:**

Your network access and the rights your company has set for you may affect your ability to get to the start page. If you have any problems getting to the start page, you should talk to your IT staff.

Basic Components of the Start Page

If you're not used to how the SharePoint Online start page is laid out, it can be hard to find your way around it. Don't worry, though; it will be very easy to use once you get the hang of it. Let's look at the start page's main parts one by one so you know what you're looking at and how to use it correctly. **Also, this is how the start page looks in general:**

1. **Search Functionality**: The search box is right at the top of your start page, making it easy to look through recently used files and websites. Furthermore, it gives you the ability to

look for other people in your group as well as other websites and files. When you use the search tool on the start page, all relevant search results from OneDrive and other sites are brought together.

2. **Site Creation Feature**: You will see an option to start creating a new site if your supervisor gives you the right powers. This will bring up a range of options that will ask you to choose the type of site you want to make, such as a current conversation site or a team site.

3. **Post Creation Capability**: Next to the button for creating a site is the option for writing new news posts, which is a useful tool for sharing project or team updates. Since this is done right from the home page, you need to choose which site you want to post the news on.

4. **Sites You're Following**: This part lists all the sites you have chosen to follow, making them easy to get to. If you want to follow a site, click the star button on the home page (or start page).

5. **Your Recent Sites**: This is a list of the sites you've been to lately. The "see all" link takes you to a full list of all of these sites.

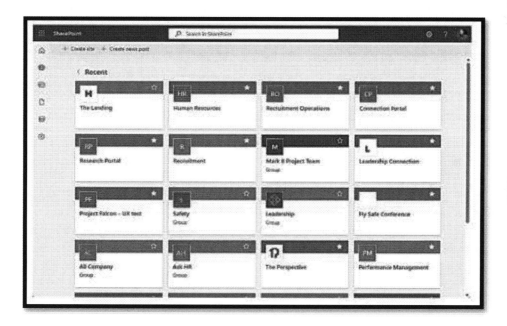

6. **Featured Links**: This section highlights links to important sites and portals that your company chooses. The option to personalize these links is open to those with Microsoft 365 manager powers.

7. **Latest Site News**: The newest information from sites you follow or visit often is shown in this news part. Additionally, selected news may be shown, made easier by the Office Graph. If there are a lot of news posts, a "see all" link lets you see the 100 most recent ones.

8. **Frequently Visited Sites**: This section shows the sites you visit often, along with new action reports for each one. If you have more than 12 sites that you visit often, a "see"

link will take you to a full list. This tool is especially helpful for quickly getting to SharePoint sites that you use a lot. Keep in mind that Microsoft Graph made this list automatically and that it cannot be changed by hand.

9. **Suggested Sites for You**: These are personalized site suggestions made based on what you've done and data from Office Graph. Keep in mind that this function can only be used if the Office Graph settings are right. Administrators can change these settings in the Microsoft 365 admin center.

10. **Saved News Posts**: The news posts you've chosen to read later are nicely filed in this area. If you click the pin icon on a news story, you can save it to read later.

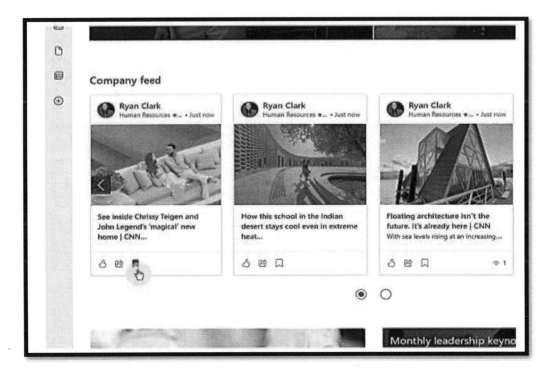

Best Practices for Using the SharePoint Start Page

Following some best practices can make it easy to find your way around and use the start page. These tips will help you get more out of SharePoint by making it easier to use, better organized, and faster.

Do's

- **Keep things easy:** You can change how your start page looks, but keep in mind that keeping it simple is important. Having a lot of stuff around will make it harder to find what you need.

- **Use the 'following' feature**: For important projects and papers, use the "**Following**" option. They will always be just a click away this way.
- **Keep your information up to date**: A lot of the time, your profile affects how you use SharePoint. To get the most up-to-date and useful information, make sure it is up-to-date.
- **Check for news and updates**. News and updates from sites you're a part of are often shown on the start page. Make it a habit to quickly read these to find any important details.

Don'ts

- **Don't ignore security rules**: Always follow the security rules set by your company. This means not giving out private information or your login information.
- **Don't sign in to SharePoint more than once**. If you're signed in on more than one device, make sure to log out of the ones you're not using. This is good for the system's security and speed.
- **Pay attention to alarms and messages**; they're there for a reason. If you don't pay attention to them, you might miss important jobs or changes.

Common Mistakes to Avoid

- **Ignoring permission levels**: SharePoint has different levels of permission for a reason. Make sure you know what you can and can't do so you don't change or delete important information by accident.
- **Not using all of SharePoint's features**: SharePoint has many features. SharePoint can be used to its fullest if you don't use tools like document files, groups, and the search function.

Version Control and Check-in/Check-out

One of the most basic features of SharePoint that you will probably use every day is "**check-in/out**." You do not have to use it. Be smart and only use it when you think it makes sense. Another part of SharePoint that can be hard to understand is the "**check-in/out**" feature. I've even seen users who check in and out all the time when they don't have to. To begin, there isn't a single way to talk about the feature. Some people say "**check in**" for it. "**Check out**" is what some people call it. Some people say "**check in-and-out**," "check-in-out," or the satisfyingly quick "**check-in-check-out**." For now, I'm going to use "**check out**" instead. We're all talking about the same thing, though. I'm not going to hide the fact that I hate check out. **Yes**, the word "**hate**" is strong. I used it for a reason. I believe that check out is a thing of the past and isn't needed in a modern office that uses **SharePoint 2013, 2016, or Online**. The idea behind it was good, but most people didn't see the small rewards. It made things more complicated than they needed to be. That's right.

How to use check out

In simple terms, checking out is like grabbing a tool that ensures you're the only person who can tinker with a file. Think of it like borrowing a book from the library – once you've checked it out, it's exclusively yours, and nobody else can make changes. Follow one of the steps below to let

SharePoint check the file out to you. When the file is checked out, you'll see a small green button in the bottom right corner of the icon (item 1 in the picture below). Also, if you show the **"Checked Out To"** tab in a library, SharePoint will let everyone know that the file is checked out to you (item 2 in the picture below).

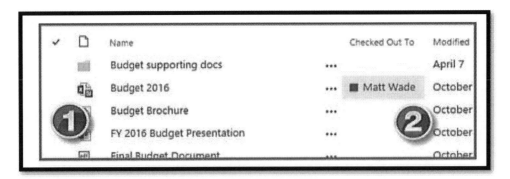

After you've finished making changes to the file, checking it back in allows you to share it with your colleagues. Simply save the file one last time and close the program. Return to the SharePoint library and confirm that the file is present, following the steps outlined below.

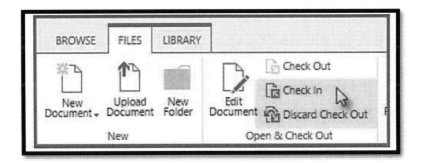

You can also delete your check out, as shown in that picture. There will be no more changes to the file after you check it out, even if you saved them. The file will go back to the way it was before you checked it out. This is a last-ditch effort if you made a lot of changes that you don't want to be used or if the file is broken and you don't want a version to be made that has the broken parts. SharePoint will ask you if you want to keep the check out after you mark the file as checked in. (I don't understand.). What's more useful is that the pop-up lets you leave a note, which can be something useful like *"Finished reviewing."* The reader can now get the file. I like the idea of notes, but I don't think anyone ever really uses them. This is likely because the option is usually only there when you check in a file.

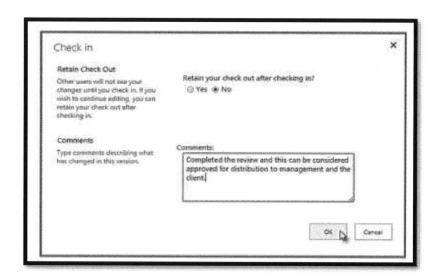

If versioning is not turned off, every time you check in a file, a new version of the file is made. (You can still use check out even if versioning is turned off.) This can help you make a new version of a file, especially if it's not an Office file.

Required check out

Document libraries don't need files to be checked out to be changed by default. It would be terrible if you had to. In a library, Site Owners can make check out mandatory by going to **Library settings > Versioning Settings > Yes** under "**Require documents to be checked out before they can be edited**?" Toggle that option to "**No**" to turn off check out.

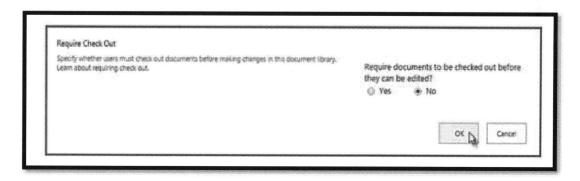

Check-out is usually linked to version history, and you can tell that's how it's supposed to work by where you turn it on and off. Please keep in mind that only the Site Owner can turn check out on and off, and only at the library level. There is no way to make all of a site's checkouts needed at once.

When to use check out

It can be helpful to use check out when you have very strict review processes and want to make sure that only the reviewer can change the file while it's going through reviews. Also, each writer needs to know a lot about how check out works because it's easy for people to get lost. Users who don't know what they're doing can make the process worse than it needs to be. Another quick and dirty way to "*lock*" a file so that no one else can change it is to check it out. There are several reasons why this might be needed. The people who don't have Site Owner access to the library and can't change rights will find it very useful and tempting. Another way to lock a file is to make it read-only, so no one can change it. This can only be done by the Site Owner.

Check out and metadata

Keep in mind that this part was made for the old version of SharePoint. There is no longer a problem with this in modern SharePoint (in SharePoint Online). If you want to add a file to a library that needs information, you'll need to check it in first. There's no way around this, but it's how things are. If you click on the "**Upload**" button above the library content or the menu, you will be asked to enter the file's information and be shown your options. Once you're done, the file will be checked in.

If you normally drag and drop files into your browser (or maybe even through File Explorer), the file(s) will upload, but you won't be asked to choose any information. The file(s) end up in the library because you checked them out. It doesn't give you any notice; it just does. Either uses the "**upload**" button or drag-and-drop to add files to a library that need information. After doing

11

either, be sure to check that the files were added correctly. I tell people to always use the **"upload"** button in libraries with needed information because this process is very hard to understand and can lead to a huge number of checked-out files.

Version History

Version history likely is one of the best tools in SharePoint. It shows you a list of all the changes that have been made to your files over time. You can see old copies of your files in version history, which also tells you how many versions there are, how big each version is, and who made each version and when. You might think that the tool your company uses to back up shared drives is good enough. That you wouldn't need anything else? Not so fast. I will give you some real-life examples of when many shared drive saves won't work, which could mean hours of extra work that you wouldn't have to do if you had just used SharePoint from the start.

Version history is generally used in two ways:

1. **Plain old version history:**
   - A straightforward method involves checking the version history in SharePoint. This is particularly handy for comparing the current version of a file with its previous iterations, providing valuable insights into changes and the file's current status.
   - It also allows you to monitor who has made alterations, offering transparency in the editing process. In case the current version turns out to be undesirable, damaged, or simply regrettable, you have the option to restore older versions.
   - This uncomplicated approach serves as an easy-to-use backup and review system, eliminating the need for IT assistance.
2. **A robust release system:**
   - Another option is a more sophisticated release system embedded in version history. This system mirrors the methodology used in software releases, endowing you with substantial control over your documents.
   - The version numbers become pivotal, guiding you through the evolution of your papers. Furthermore, you can restrict access to specific file types, providing a level of control suitable for business settings. While highly effective in such environments, it requires a more intricate setup and ongoing maintenance.

Why version history is useful

Certainly, navigating through old versions becomes quite a challenge, and it might induce a sense of unease, especially when relying on shared drives for file storage in a company. Unlike SharePoint's user-friendly version history, the process in shared drives can be less straightforward. In this scenario, your reliance is often on a backup system, typically scheduled to run daily at midnight, or, if fortunate, more frequently managed by the IT group. Some organizations, operating at a higher level of caution, might back up shared drives every hour, retaining files for a day, followed by daily backups for a week, and weekly backups for a month. However, this level of diligence is not universal due to resource constraints. It's important to note that this backup strategy doesn't offer real-time recovery. For instance, if you're working on a file regularly within an hourly timeframe and accidentally overwrite it, the last backup made within that hour becomes your sole recourse. This means that despite multiple saves during that hour, only the final version is retrievable. One inadvertent click could potentially result in the loss of a substantial amount of time and work. It underscores the importance of carefully managing files and being aware of the limitations of the backup system in place.

Absolutely, the reliance on shared drive backups can be somewhat uncertain. The backup frequency, duration, and the specific times they occur are often set by the IT staff, leaving users in the dark about the intricacies of the system. Access to these backups may also require the submission of a trouble ticket, adding an extra layer of complexity. On the other hand, SharePoint offers a more dynamic solution through its "version history" feature. This feature creates a new copy of a file in four key scenarios: every time you save, check in, update, or collaborate with others (with versions generated every half hour during collaborative work). What sets it apart is the flexibility it provides – versions are created when you think they should be, putting the control in your hands rather than relying solely on system backups. The ability to travel back in time and access any version of a file is a significant advantage. You can even choose to revert to an earlier version and designate it as the current one. The flexibility extends to deciding how long your files will be retained, tracking who has accessed them, and rectifying mistakes seamlessly. It's a user-centric approach that empowers individuals to manage and safeguard their work effectively.

How version history works

First, make sure it's turned on: Make sure that your document library has version history turned on.

When versions are created

Every time you do one of the following, versions will be made:

- **Saving in the Client App:**
  - Every time you open a file in the client application and click the "Save" button, a fresh version is created. This method applies specifically to client apps and differs from the process in browser-based Office Web Apps (OWA) or Office Online (OO).
- **Making Changes in Browser App (OWA/OO):**
  - In OWA/OO, where there isn't a traditional "Save" button, a new version is generated every thirty minutes while actively making changes. To trigger this, close OWA/OO (your changes are instantly saved but not versioned yet), check out the file, and then promptly check it back in. This sequence initiates the creation of a new version.
- **Deleting a File:**
  - Adding a file to the document library with an identical name to an existing file prompts SharePoint to create a new version rather than overwriting the old one. For example, if you upload a file named "Movie1.mp4" when there's already a file with that name; SharePoint will inquire if you want to replace the file. Opting to do so results in the generation of a new version, even if the content is different.
- **Checking In a File:**
  - Checking in a file after checking it out, irrespective of whether changes were made, triggers the creation of a new version. This provides users with the flexibility to update the version even if no modifications were applied during the checkout period.

Accessing the versions of a file

These are the three most popular ways to see a file's version history: Certainly, accessing the version history in SharePoint can be accomplished through various methods:

1. **Right-Click Method:**
   - Right-click on the file name to reveal a menu.
   - Click on "Version history" from the options presented.
2. **Checkbox and Ribbon Method:**
   - Check the box next to the file name.
   - Navigate to the "File" tab on the ribbon.
   - Click on "Version history" to access the file's version history.
3. **Hover and Ellipses Method:**
   - Hover over the file name until an ellipses (...) appears.
   - Click on the ellipses (...).
   - Another set of ellipses (...) will appear in the hover box.
   - Click on the second set of ellipses (...) and choose "Version history" from the options provided.

The version history pane

The version history box will show you the most recent and older versions of your file after you follow the steps above. The data will be shown in a table style, showing **1)** the version number (going down), **2)** the date and time stamp that shows when the version was made, **3)** who made the change, **4)** the file size at the time of the change, and **5)** any notes that the author made. The list will also show any information that has been changed. If you click on the column title (like **"No.," "Modified," "Modified By**," etc.), you can put the columns in alphabetical order. This is helpful if you want to see all the changes that a certain person made or if the file size stayed about the same between versions, which means that not much changed.

Integrating SharePoint with Microsoft 365 Apps and Third-Party Systems

Integrating SharePoint with Microsoft 365 Apps, which used to be called Office 365, is a key part of Microsoft's plan to make its Office suite work together smoothly. SharePoint's powerful document management and collaboration tools are now combined with the well-known and powerful Microsoft 365 Apps tools. This makes a single environment for businesses. What else can SharePoint work with?

Products from the Microsoft 365 Suite

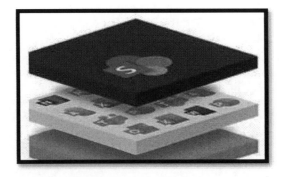

Since SharePoint is seamlessly integrated into the Microsoft 365 suite, users logged into their SharePoint accounts can effortlessly connect with content across various MS 365 applications and within SharePoint itself. However, for processes specific to a company or for displaying particular data from other Microsoft 365 products, additional customized processes may be required. For example, when it comes to conducting polls, SharePoint lists are a reliable choice. While crafting a unique list may take some time, it's a bit more intricate when attempting to distribute it beyond the company. In such cases, Microsoft Forms proves to be a more efficient solution. This service enables users to swiftly create well-organized poll forms that can be easily disseminated. The beauty lies in the fact that the form seamlessly links to SharePoint, ensuring that the responses are transmitted to the intranet. Once there, the data can be categorized into groups and harnessed by other applications as needed. This interoperability enhances the functionality of Microsoft 365 tools, providing tailored solutions for diverse organizational needs.

Software Products outside the Microsoft 365 Suite

Depending on your goals, you can connect the common tools that your workers use to SharePoint to make the processes that involve these tools more efficient.

Client Relationship Management Systems (CRMs)

SharePoint seamlessly integrates with Customer Relationship Management (CRM) systems, streamlining the management of paperwork associated with marketing and sales. The meticulous task of completing plans, contracts, or deals becomes more efficient when SharePoint is interconnected with CRM. By linking SharePoint to CRM, sales and marketing teams gain the ability to leverage CRM data instantly, incorporating it into document templates whenever there's a need to generate a new document for a client. This integration significantly accelerates the document creation process while minimizing the likelihood of errors. Furthermore, users of CRM can conveniently store documents directly in SharePoint. This not only optimizes storage within the CRM system but also contributes to cost reduction associated with CRM storage. Additionally, the integration allows users to keep track of different versions of documents, ensuring that a comprehensive history is maintained. This collaborative approach between SharePoint and CRM enhances the overall efficiency of sales and marketing processes, offering a more streamlined and organized workflow.

Enterprise Resource Planning Systems (ERPs)

When SharePoint is used with ERP software, it adds value and makes it easier to handle data from different people in a company. For example, a partner or user of a business can post bills, delivery slips, and receipts to SharePoint. These documents will then be instantly identified, parsed, and uploaded to the right files in an ERP system.

Human Resources Planning Systems

Integrating SharePoint with HR planning tools makes sure that the right information gets to the right workers at the right time. When used with an HR system, SharePoint gives workers secure access to their records. On the website, workers can change their personal information, do performance reviews, see and book their annual leave, or look at their payslip.

IT Helpdesks

When an IT helpdesk is linked to SharePoint, it lets users do things on their own and quickly fixes problems. SharePoint lets workers use forms that have already been filled out to quickly make help desk tickets with accurate accounts of incidents. Employees can also check SharePoint to see how their help tickets are going. Also, IT professionals can make guides for workers and keep knowledge bases in sync when SharePoint and IT helpdesks are linked together.

Digital Asset Management Systems

It takes a lot of time to look for and add relevant media content from a DAM when making news stories, slideshows, and other materials to share on an intranet. When SharePoint is connected to a DAM, it makes managing and sharing information easier. Picturepark, a company that makes content management software, connected their DAM to SharePoint to give their customers a one-tab experience. For the first time, clients can now find digital assets from Picturepark's library in SharePoint and use them in online content they make.

Project Management Systems

When tasks are synced with project management tools, SharePoint makes team performance clearer and speeds up work. First, workers can use a PM system in SharePoint to find their jobs and keep track of how they're doing. Second, SharePoint can be used as a place for a task management system to store information. When workers work with papers and files as part of their job, tasks can be made immediately for items that are chosen in SharePoint.

Other Integrations

As needed, SharePoint can be easily expanded to send information and files saved on a website to other systems or to add data from outside SharePoint. With most third-party systems, they can be linked to a SharePoint site if they accept connections. When the SharePoint Framework (SPFx) is used, integration services for SharePoint let you use ready-made connections and make your integration cases.

Means of Integration

A business can connect SharePoint to another system in some ways, based on the available tools and the system itself.

Connectors

Microsoft AppSource is the best place to look for links for SharePoint that work with well-known solutions that are not part of the Microsoft 365 family. If there isn't a ready-to-use app that works for a company, they can have a unique connection made for their use.

Microsoft Power Platform

Within the Microsoft 365 ecosystem, the Microsoft Power Platform serves as a comprehensive suite, bringing together tools designed for data analysis, workflow automation, and the creation of new applications based on data and processes. This platform proves invaluable by seamlessly integrating various Microsoft 365 applications, including SharePoint, into a cohesive environment. **To access the features of the Power Platform, companies are required to acquire a Power Platform license from Microsoft.**

1. **Power Automate:**
   - Power Automate facilitates the automation of processes by establishing connections between SharePoint and other applications. It boasts compatibility with over 300 data sources, encompassing popular Microsoft 365 apps and even those outside the Microsoft 365 suite. This versatility empowers users to create automated workflows that span across a diverse range of applications.
2. **Power BI:**
   - Power BI plays a crucial role in gathering and presenting data from the Microsoft Power Platform's data platform and other Microsoft 365 products. While the data can be visualized within the Power BI app, a special web part allows for seamless sharing within SharePoint. Additionally, personalized results can be stored on an intranet, enhancing collaboration and accessibility.
3. **Power Apps:**
   - Power Apps provides a suite of tools that enables users to swiftly develop custom business applications and link them to various data sources, including SharePoint files and lists. Moreover, SharePoint serves as a repository for documents associated with these applications. This integration enhances the flexibility of creating tailored business apps while leveraging the robust capabilities of SharePoint.

Understanding SharePoint Sites and Hierarchy

A site in SharePoint is a group of pages, lists, libraries, apps, settings, features, and rights that are set up in a hierarchy1. Within SharePoint, the order of sites is like a tree: each site can have many child sites, and each child site can have its child sites.

Introduction to SharePoint information architecture

For an intranet, hub, or site to be smart and work well, the information design must be well thought out and carried out. To make a good information design, the first thing you need to do is know your users and help them find the things they need to do their jobs in the way that makes the most sense to them. As a bonus, information design helps boost user acceptance, happiness, and efficiency while lowering IT costs, information overload, and security and compliance risks.

Information architecture elements in SharePoint

What is information architecture? It's how you name and organize your content, as well as how people use that material to complete tasks. Navigation, search, site structure, taxonomy, and security are all parts of information design that are used on websites. The modern information design of SharePoint also includes ways to make sure that the right content gets to the right people and that your company's content safety rules are followed. **Six main parts of information design have to do with finding your way around in SharePoint:**

- **Global navigational structure**: This is the main way that people can find their way around your SharePoint property and the way that you set up your sites so that people can find information, like the homepage of your intranet.
- **Structure and order of hubs**: Hubs let you group topics, tasks, and contents that are similar together.
- **Local site and page browsing structure**: This refers to how information is organized on each site and page so that users can easily find what they're looking for or read.
- **Metadata architecture**: Metadata affects the framework of search and viewing, as well as rule-following and storage rules.
- **Search experiences**—how your users "**consume**" information design, not just look around.
- **Personalized content experiences**: how certain users and groups of users are shown certain material.

It takes enough planning to come up with the best layout for hubs, sites, and pages. It's also necessary to know about the subject, the material, the user experience, design methods, and Microsoft SharePoint best practices. Information design is a process that never ends, even if you have a good plan. Groups, people, and tasks all change over time. You'll learn more about your users over time, which will let you make changes that make information easier to find.

Understand your role and how to collaborate

It's best for your organization's information architecture when people with a variety of jobs work together on the intranet. For example, intranet owners, departmental business owners, IT managers, and hub owners should all be able to work together. Find out more about how each job helps plan, carry out, and oversee the ongoing upkeep of an organization's information architecture.

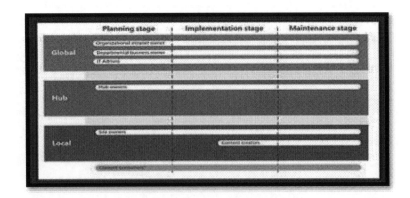

- **Organization intranet owner(s):** The organizational intranet owner(s) make decisions and coordinate the general direction and work of your company's intranet. They are made up of people with different job roles. Owners of an organization's intranet work with business owners (departments) and IT administrators to set up both global and hub-level routing. The people who run an organization's intranet will spend most of their time planning and setting up global and hub-level routing.
- **Departmental business owners**: These people are in charge of big parts of the company, like engineers, human resources, and marketing. The owners of business units within a company work with the owners of the intranet to make sure that their part of the business is well reflected in global and hub navigation. Early on in the planning process, departmental business owners should be brought in to make sure that the goals of both the business and the users are met.
- **IT administrators**: These people work with the owners of an organization's intranet and the business owners of different departments to set up high-level navigable structures like the start page and hubs. IT administrators also help put in place rules for how sites are made and how they are used. As the business grows and changes, IT administrators help plan, set up, and keep up with the information design.
- **Hub owners**—These people are in charge of the material, branding, rights, and navigational features for hubs in your company's intranet. During the lifetime of your company's intranet design, hub owners work with departmental business owners and IT administrators to plan, build, and run hubs.
- **Site owners**: They are in charge of the content, logos, rights, and access for their sites. Site owners can connect their sites to hubs if the hub owner lets them. This depends on the needs of the business and the users.
- **Content creators**—it's the job of content creators to keep the site's material up to date and to post news. Someone who makes content should be able to make changes to sites and pages as a site member. In the planning and running stages, content writers work with site owners as a team.
- **Content consumers** —Content consumers are not included in the counts because they are not people who use and view material on any of the three levels of browsing. Intranet owners, departmental business owners, hub owners, and site owners should regularly talk to content consumers, especially when planning, to make sure that users can find and use the right content.

Guiding principle: the world is flat

A tiered system of site collections and subsites is often used to build a classic SharePoint layout. Navigation, rights, and site designs are passed down from one site collection to the next. This structure can be rigid and hard to keep up once it's built. Subsites aren't suggested in the new version of SharePoint. Plan to make a separate site for each topic, job, or unit of work in the "flat" world of modern SharePoint. This will make it easy to share responsibility and control for each group of content, and it will also help you move sites around in your browsing design without breaking links. Also, you can quickly close or delete a site with little effect when a topic is no longer needed.

With the new flat world, you have some information design tools that you can use to link sites and content:

- Use **"roll up"** web parts like News, Highlighted content, or Sites to show content from other sites on top of content on your site.
- Put internal links to more information about a subject to give your reader more details (as shown in the last bullet point).
- Make sure your site's navigation has clear links to similar sites.
- Use hubs to connect groups of sites that are related.

Levels of navigation

When you use modern SharePoint, you should think about three levels of navigation:

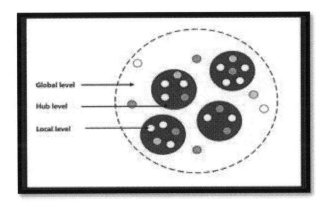

- Global navigation for the entire collection of sites that comprise your intranet
- Hub navigation for groups of related sites
- Local navigation of an individual site

Global navigation

A lot of intranets have access at the top that stays the same on all sites. You can make a visual story for your intranet's navigation that links all the sites, information, and tools your users need to get work done with global navigation. **Each company has its own rules about what should be in global navigation, but some of the most common names for these ideas are:**

- Home
- About Us
- News
- Working Here/Work Resources/Administrative Services/Administration

- Operations/Operations Services
- Pay & Benefits
- Life & Career
- Locations
- Policies & Procedures/Tools & Resources/Safety & Security

The point of global navigation is to make it easier to browse information. To make the most of the space they have, global navigation links usually lead to main category navigation pages, sub-links, or a giant menu. This gives users enough information to find the content they need. It's hard to make labels that are both complete and useful for world travel because the context has to be broad. You should try your suggested navigation to make sure that people like it if you want to use global navigation. The SharePoint app bar on your home page lets you navigate around the site as a whole. To let people around the world find your site, you need a home page. Every site and page has global access on the left side.

Hub navigation

SharePoint hubs help group sites that are linked by idea, project, department, division, or area. Hubs make it easier to find news and other activities on sites that are linked. They also let you use the same layout, branding, and site structure across all sites that are connected, and you can look across all of them. Planning the hub navigation is one of the most important things that need to be done when planning a hub.

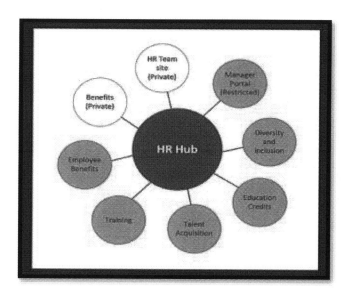

On each site, the hub navigation shows up just below the suite bar, above the local navigation. The site that is said to be the hub is where hub routing is set up. It's set by the hub owner and shared by all the sites that are linked to it.

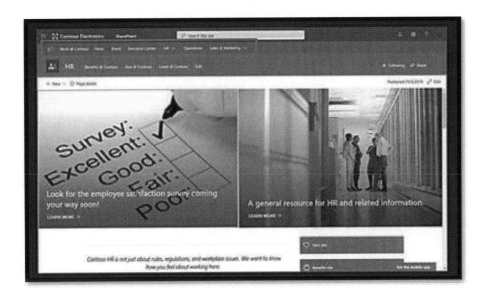

At a time, each site can only be part of one hub. However, you can link hubs together using navigation links and linked hubs as part of your navigation experience.

Local navigation

People can see the same navigation on every page of your site, which is called "**local navigation**." On team sites, the "**quick launch**" area on the left side of the page is where you can find this menu. On contact sites, the local menu bar is at the top of the page. Every page of your site has local access. Visitors can stay on one site longer if they can go back and forth between pages and information on different sites. Think about how people might want to explore your information and use local browsing to help them do that. Some examples of local navigation links that could be on a travel site are those below. These links can help people who are looking at the site to find out "***what am I allowed to do***?" as well as people who are looking at the site to plan their trip (before, during, and after).

- **Travel guidelines**
  - Air
  - Car
  - Ground Transportation
  - Hotel
  - Train
- **Before you go**
  - Travel approval
  - Booking service
- **During your trip**
  - Travel safety
  - Itinerary changes

- **After you return**
  - Expense reporting
  - Trip reports

Where you'll see local navigation elements:

Team site navigation

Communication site navigation

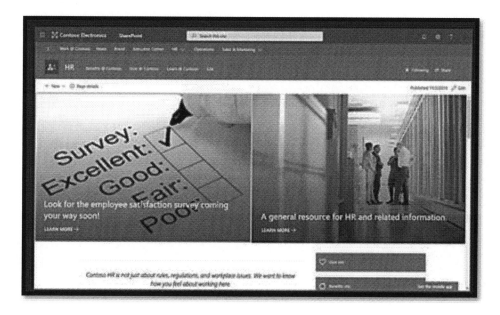

Sites

Your intranet and portals are made up of communication and team sites that give you more access to the site's pages, lists, and libraries. Microsoft 365 groups are part of current SharePoint team sites that make information design easy to set up and keep up to date. Microsoft 365 groups are a membership service that makes it easy to set rights for hubs and sites. They also offer extra features for SharePoint team sites and Microsoft Teams. You can give a group of people access to collaboration tools like Planner, OneNote, SharePoint team sites, and more with Microsoft 365 groups. You can only use M365 groups on SharePoint team sites.

Pages

You can use News, Highlighted content, or Sites web parts, which are interactive web parts that can instantly change content from other sites and pages, on pages in team or communication sites. Each site's page tells a story.

There are three main types of pages on your sites:

- The **home pages**, where you'll give a summary of your site's content and tell people what they can expect to find there.
- **Navigation pages**: These are pages that help the person decide where they want to go next by giving them options or summaries of information.
- The reader's journey concludes on **destination pages**. You will put information here for people to read, print, or download. You can make a secondary page if your main page has a lot of information or if you want to give more information about a complicated subject.

Most people don't read every word on a web page or even scroll to the bottom, so you need to think about how you arrange the information on each page. Make sure the most important information is at the top of the page. This is the information that your readers need to understand your message. You can keep adding helpful but not necessary information as the page goes on. This is like putting your summary or ending at the beginning of your work instead of the end. To make your pages easier to read, divide them up with parts, headers, and bullet points.

Navigational elements

These are things like the giant menu, the waterfall menu, and the bottom menu that helps with navigation. Inline links and buttons are examples of secondary navigational features.

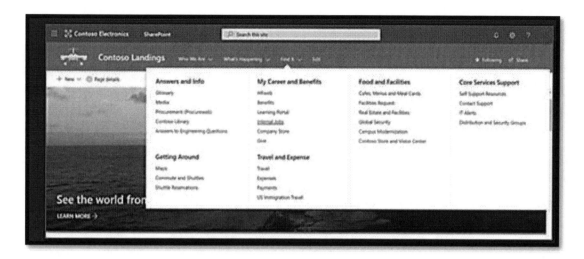

Personalization elements

Audience targeting- This helps the best content reach the right people. By setting up audience targeting, SharePoint web parts, page libraries, and navigational links will show certain material more prominently to certain groups of people.

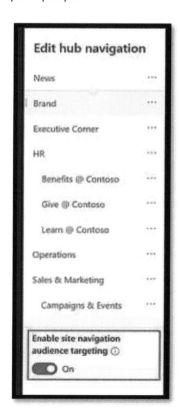

- **Information barriers**: Information barriers are rules in Microsoft 365 that a compliance admin can set up to stop users from working together and speaking with each other. This is helpful if, say, one division is in charge of information that shouldn't be shared with certain other divisions, or if one division needs to be kept from working together with anyone outside of their division. Information walls are commonly used in businesses that have to follow strict rules, like those in banking, law, and government.
- **Multilingual considerations** —If the people who work for your company are from different backgrounds, you might want to make material on your intranet sites available in more than one language. The user can choose which language to see site navigation, the site title, and the site description in the user interface. On communication sites, you can also offer pages and news posts that you translate and show in the user's chosen language.

As many languages as you offer, the site name, menu, and bottom must all be translated by hand for them to show up in those languages. Take the example of a communication site that you set to English as the default language and also made available in Spanish and German. The name and description of your site are set in the usual language when you make it. In this case, English. You can change the site's name and description even after it's been made. Then you write the English text for the menu nodes and the bottom. Once the site is set up in English, a user whose first language is Spanish changes and turns the title, description, menu, and bottom material by hand into Spanish. A user who chooses German as their main language does the same thing for German. The information will be displayed for every user of those languages once it has been translated.

Metadata architecture

Columns and content types stand out as pivotal elements for structuring pages and documents within your SharePoint site. Leveraging metadata allows users to efficiently search for material within lists or libraries while providing sorting and filtering capabilities. The incorporation of columns, particularly in the Site Pages library, facilitates the utilization of highlighted content web parts, fostering connections between pages based on shared information.

Folders as an Organizational Tool

Folders offer an additional method for organizing information in documents, albeit with certain constraints. While folders provide a fixed organizational structure, making changes is not always straightforward. Although folders can contribute to the smooth and secure operation of document libraries, it's crucial to be mindful of their limitations. Organizing information with more than two levels of nesting in folder layouts can impede user navigation and should be avoided for optimal accessibility.

Multiple Document Libraries for Enhanced Organization

Rather than relying solely on the default Documents library, consider employing multiple document libraries on a site. Each site is equipped with one library, but the addition of topic-specific libraries and site columns can elevate content organization. This approach mitigates the need for extensive folder nesting, promoting a more streamlined and user-friendly experience. By incorporating site columns and distinct libraries, you enhance the overall organization of content within your intranet sites, reducing the reliance on intricate folder structures.

Search experiences

You've probably already spent money on information architecture. Search can help people find content when they don't know where it is in your design. Additionally, it aids user discovery of previously undiscovered material. In search, you can use tools like symbols, notes, Q&A, floor plans, and places to help users find material and improve search results.

CHAPTER 2

GETTING STARTED WITH SHAREPOINT

Accessing SharePoint: Web Interface and Desktop Applications

Accessing SharePoint via Web Browser

Using an online browser to connect to SharePoint is an easy way to get to your sites and use the many information and collaboration tools it provides. SharePoint is made to work with all major web platforms, so you can use it whether you like Internet Explorer, Google Chrome, or Mozilla Firefox. For example, we will look at how to open SharePoint in Internet Explorer, Google Chrome, and Mozilla Firefox in this part.

1. Open your browser.
2. Type the URL for your SharePoint site into the search bar. Such as **"https://yoursharepointsite.com".**
3. Press **"Enter"** to bring up the LinkedIn site.
4. You might be asked to enter your password information. To get into SharePoint, enter your account and password.

You will be able to see all of your SharePoint site's tools and material once you are logged in.

Accessing SharePoint on Mobile Devices

These days, life moves quickly, so being able to access SharePoint while you're out and about is important for staying connected and busy. With more people using smartphones and computers, SharePoint has changed to make it easier to use on mobile devices. We will talk about how to use SharePoint on mobile devices, such as how to install the SharePoint Mobile App and use a mobile browser to access SharePoint.

Installing SharePoint Mobile App

The SharePoint Mobile App can be downloaded for both iOS and Android devices so that you can use SharePoint on the go. The SharePoint Mobile App makes it easy to view your SharePoint sites, documents, and lists on your phone by giving you a user-friendly layout that is designed for mobile devices. **The SharePoint Mobile App can be put on your phone in this way:**

1. On your phone, open the App Store (iOS) or the Google Play Store (Android).
2. Type **"SharePoint"** into the search bar.
3. Find the Microsoft Corporation official SharePoint Mobile App and tap on it.
4. Tap the **"Get"** or **"Install"** button to get the app on your device and install it.

5. Open the SharePoint Mobile App once the download is done.
6. You will be asked to sign in with the information for your SharePoint account. To log in, type in your login and password.

With the SharePoint Mobile App, you can easily move around your SharePoint sites, view documents, join talks, and work with your team while you're on the go thanks to its mobile-friendly design. It gives you access to all of SharePoint's power, so you can stay connected and get work done from anywhere.

Accessing SharePoint via Mobile Browser

You can still use a mobile browser to view SharePoint on your phone or tablet if you don't want to install the SharePoint Mobile App. This is how you can do it:

1. Find the web browser on your phone or tablet.
2. In the search bar, type in the URL for your SharePoint site. Such as "https://yoursharepointsite.com".
3. Press "**Enter**" to bring up the LinkedIn site.
4. If asked, give your login information to get into SharePoint.

You can look at your SharePoint sites, get to papers, and do other things once you are logged in, just like you would on a desktop browser. The mobile version, on the other hand, is designed to work best with smaller screens and touch interactions, so the viewing experience may be different from the PC version.

Logging in to SharePoint

Making an account on SharePoint is the first thing you need to do to access and use all of its powerful features and functions. We will talk about how to make a SharePoint account and change your password in this part.

Creating a SharePoint Account

The first thing you need to do with SharePoint is make an account. Start by setting up your account in a few easy steps:

1. **Go to the SharePoint Sign-Up Page**: Open the online browser you like best and go to the SharePoint sign-up page.
2. **Press the "Get started for free" button**: You will see an option to start for free on the sign-up page. If you click on it, the process of making an account will begin.
3. **Type in your email address**: Give a real email address that you can get to. This email address will be linked to your SharePoint account and used to send you messages.

4. **Enter your personal information**. SharePoint will ask you for simple information about yourself, like your name and the name of your company. To finish the registration process, make sure the information you give is correct.
5. **Make a unique username and password**. For your SharePoint account, make a strong password and a unique username. For extra protection, make sure your password has a mix of capital and lowercase letters, numbers, and special characters.
6. **Agree to the rules**: Read the SharePoint terms and conditions and, if you agree, check the box to show that you understand them.
7. **Check your email address**. Once you're done registering, SharePoint will send a proof email to the address you gave. To prove your account, go to your email and click on the link that says "Verification."

Excellent work! Your SharePoint account has been successfully set up. Let's move on to the next subject and learn how to change your password if you forget it.

Resetting SharePoint Password

We all forget our passwords from time to time. Don't worry if you can't get into your SharePoint account because you forgot your password. There is an easy way to change your password in SharePoint. **To get back in, do these things:**

1. **Click on the link to log in to SharePoint**: Start up your online browser and go to the SharePoint login page.
2. **Click on "Forgot Password"**: You will see an option to change your password on the login screen. To start the process of getting your password back, click on the "Forgot Password" link.
3. **Type in your email address**: Give the email address that goes with your SharePoint account. This should be the email address you used when you first made the account.
4. **Confirm your identity**: To keep your account safe, SharePoint will ask you to confirm your identity. This could mean answering security questions, entering a verification code that was sent to your phone or email, or using some other way of proof.
5. **Change your password**: You will be able to change your password once your name has been confirmed. Select a new password that meets the security requirements, and then accept the change.
6. **Enter your new password to log in**. Once you've changed your password, you can now use the new information to access your SharePoint account.

Make sure you pick a strong password that is easy for you to remember but hard for other people to figure out. Try not to use common words or personal details so that people can quickly connect with you.

Using SharePoint Discussion Boards

SharePoint discussion boards give team members a place to have deep talks, share their ideas, and ask for other people's opinions. They are like virtual meeting rooms where people on the team can talk about things, ask questions, and give helpful feedback.

Here are the steps you need to take to use SharePoint discussion boards:

1. Go to the website where you want to make a discussion board.
2. Press the gear button next to **"Settings"** and pick **"Add an app."**
3. Look for **"Discussion Board"** on your site and click on it to add it.
4. Choose a name for the discussion board and click **"New."**
5. Once the discussion board is set up, you can start new conversations or join ones that are already going on.
6. To begin a new discussion, select **"New Discussion"** from the menu.
7. Choose a topic for the discussion and give a full explanation.
8. You can add tags or connect files if you want to make it easy to sort and find conversations.
9. To make the discussion public, click the **"Post"** button.

By offering a place for open and honest conversation, SharePoint discussion boards promote collaboration. They let people on the team share their ideas, get comments, and work together to solve problems. With discussion boards, you can use your team's knowledge and experience to help others, which will improve collaboration and lead to new ideas.

Troubleshooting SharePoint Access Issues

SharePoint is an effective tool for document management and collaboration, but like any other piece of technology, it can occasionally run into access problems that impede work. We will look at some common SharePoint access problems and talk about good ways to fix them in this part.

Common SharePoint Access Errors

1. **"Access Denied" Error**: The scary **"Access Denied"** message is one of the most common SharePoint login problems. This mistake usually happens when a user doesn't have the right permissions to view or change a document or website. It might be annoying, but there are things you can do to fix it.
2. **Check Permissions Again**: Make sure that your user account has the right access given to it. Talk to your SharePoint supervisor for help if you think you should be able to see a certain document or site.
3. **Ask for entry**: If you don't have the right permissions, you can ask the owner of the document or site for entry directly. It's easy to ask for entry in SharePoint, and the owner can review the request and give rights as needed.

4. **Check the Site Collection Administrator**. If you get **"*Access Denied*"** problems even when you're on the main site, it might be because you don't have enough rights at the site collection level. Check your job as a site collection master by contacting your SharePoint supervisor.

5. **"Page Not Found" Error**: The **"*Page Not Found*"** error, which is also called **error 404**, strikes often. This mistake shows up when the SharePoint site can't find the page or document that was asked for. Here are some things you can try to fix it:

6. **Check the URL**: Make sure the URL is right and leads to the page or document you want by checking it twice. Typos or bad URLs can easily cause a **"*Page Not Found*"** message.

7. **Check Permissions**: If the URL is exact but you still get an error, you might not have the right permissions to see the page or document you want to see. Check your rights, and if you need to, ask for entry.

8. **Bring back wiped Items**: Sometimes, the page or document may have been wiped by accident. There is a place in SharePoint called **"*Recycle Bin*"** where removed things can be found again. Check the recycle bin and put anything back that you need to.

9. **"Server Unavailable" Error**: Sometimes when a user tries to join SharePoint, they get the "Server Unavailable" error. Based on this warning, it looks like the SharePoint server is having technical issues right now. You can do the following:

   a. **Check the SharePoint Status**: To see if there are any known server problems or repair tasks, go to the SharePoint service status page or call your SharePoint administrator.

   b. **Clear Your Browser Cache**: If you run into brief problems that might be causing the **"Server Unavailable"** error, clearing your browser cache can help fix them. Just clear the cookies in your browser's settings.

   c. **Try a Different Browser**: If the problem still happens, use a different browser to view SharePoint. Problems with certain browsers can sometimes make it impossible to view SharePoint.

Resolving SharePoint Access Problems

- **Contact SharePoint Administrator**: If you've tried all of the above debugging steps and are still having trouble, it's time to get help from your SharePoint administrator. They are qualified and have the power to look into the issue more deeply and offer an answer.

- **Look at the SharePoint logs**. SharePoint creates logs that can help you figure out problems with access. The people in charge of SharePoint can look through these logs to find any error messages or warning signs that might help them figure out what's wrong.

- **Check SharePoint**: Always make sure that the changes and fixes you use for SharePoint are the most recent ones. Microsoft offers updates daily to fix known problems and make the system more stable. Updating your SharePoint setting can help keep entry issues from happening.

- **Do a rights Audit**: Doing a rights audit regularly can help you find any errors or misconfigurations that might be preventing entry. Check and change users' permissions regularly to make sure they have the right amount of access.

Best Practices for SharePoint Access

For collaboration and document handling, SharePoint is a robust tool with many features. However, it is important to follow best practices for entry to make sure that your SharePoint experience is smooth and safe. These two important parts of SharePoint access will be talked about in this section: keeping SharePoint access safe and making it work better.

Securing SharePoint Access

Security should be the most important thing when it comes to SharePoint access. The best ways to make sure that only approved users can get to your SharePoint site and its tools are listed below.

1. **User Authentication**: Make sure that users who access SharePoint are who they say they are by putting in place strong security methods. You can do this with tools like single sign-on systems, multi-factor security, or integrating Active Directory.
2. **Role-Based Access Control: (RBAC)** Role-based access control lets you give different people or groups different rights and levels of access. This makes sure that users can only get the tools they need to do their jobs, which lowers the risk of someone else getting in without permission.
3. **Periodic Access Checks**: Make sure that user rights are up-to-date and match their current jobs and responsibilities by conducting periodic access checks. For people who no longer need access to certain SharePoint tools, remove or modify their rights.
4. **Secure External Sharing**: Set up secure external sharing tools if you need to share SharePoint resources with partners or people from outside your company. This can include things like letting guests in, sharing links that expire, or making outside users sign in with their passwords.
5. **Data Loss Prevention (DLP):** Set up DLP rules to keep private data from getting shared or leaked by accident. DLP rules can help SharePoint users find and stop the sharing of private data like credit card numbers or social security numbers.
6. **Monitoring and Auditing**: Check the SharePoint access logs regularly to find any strange activities or possible security holes. This can help find security issues quickly and help fix them.

Optimizing SharePoint Access Performance

For a smooth user experience, it's important to do more than just protect SharePoint access. By following these best practices, you can make sure that SharePoint works quickly and correctly.

1. **Set up information Delivery Networks (CDNs).** Use CDNs to send SharePoint information to computers that are in different places. This makes SharePoint tools faster and more available, especially for users in different parts of the world.

2. **Turn on Caching**: Turn on SharePoint's built-in caching feature to keep information that users view often closer to them. This makes the SharePoint system less busy and speeds up responses.
3. **Improve Images and Files**: To make images and files shared to SharePoint smaller without losing quality, compress and improve them. This speeds up the time it takes for SharePoint pages to load and uses less network traffic.
4. **Use Content Approval**: Make sure that only accepted and checked material is released by setting up content approval processes for SharePoint libraries. This keeps missing or wrong information from getting out there, which raises the standard and trustworthiness of all SharePoint material.
5. **Manage Big Lists**: If you have a lot of lists in SharePoint, you should use sorting and filters to make list views run faster. It might also be a good idea to use views with selective filters to limit the amount of info that people see.
6. **Regular Maintenance**: Do regular maintenance jobs like optimizing databases, getting rid of sites or libraries that aren't being used, and storing material that is no longer relevant. This keeps SharePoint going easily and stops it from getting slower over time.

Understanding Document Libraries

A document library in SharePoint is a place where you can store and organize files. You can use it like a virtual filing box whenever you want, as long as you have an internet link. With SharePoint's document library, you can make, post, update, and share files with your team right away. You can work together on projects, see different versions, and keep all of your papers in one place. Not only does using Document Libraries save you time and effort, but it also lets you use powerful search tools and sort documents. Setting rights, organizing documents, and having version control are some of the basic features of SharePoint Document Library that make it a useful tool for managing documents. By using Document Libraries, we can make sure that all of our team members can see and use our material, which improves collaboration and productivity. Modern SharePoint Document Libraries offer advanced features that improve collaboration and efficiency, such as process automation, co-authoring, and OneDrive syncing.

Planning Your Document Library in SharePoint

Creating a well-structured Document Library in SharePoint involves careful consideration of the company's requirements, designing an appropriate structure, and optimizing information and views for easy document retrieval and organization. **Establishing a framework that is scalable and efficient entails several key steps:**

1. **Planning the Information Architecture:**
    - Begin by strategizing the overall information architecture. Understand the types of documents the company deals with, how they are related, and how users will interact with them. This planning phase lays the foundation for a coherent structure.

2. **Establishing a Hierarchical Structure:**
   - Design a hierarchical structure that reflects the logical organization of documents. This structure aids in intuitive navigation and ensures that related documents are grouped logically, facilitating ease of access.
3. **Determining the Type of Library:**
   - Choose the appropriate type of library based on the nature of the documents. SharePoint offers various library types, such as document libraries, picture libraries, and form libraries, each tailored to specific content needs.
4. **Using Metadata for Document Discoverability and Categorization:**
   - Leverage metadata to enhance document discoverability. Define metadata fields that allow users to categorize and filter documents efficiently, making it simpler to locate specific information within the library.
5. **Creating Document Sets:**
   - Utilize document sets to group related documents together. This feature is particularly useful when dealing with projects or cases that involve multiple documents. Document sets provide a container for related content, improving organization and collaboration.
6. **Implementing Version Control:**
   - Implement version control to manage document revisions effectively. This ensures that the latest version is easily accessible while maintaining a version history that can be referred to if needed.
7. **Considering Security and Permissions:**
   - Address security and permissions to control access to documents. Define user roles and permissions based on organizational needs, safeguarding sensitive information and ensuring that only authorized individuals can access and modify documents.

Creating and Managing Sharepoint Document Libraries

Automatic Creation of Default Document Library

When you create a new SharePoint site, it comes with a document library called "Documents" that works perfectly with the site's home page. This feature is automatically created and can be used as a starting point for files and documents. It can be improved by adding more document libraries to help organize and handle a wider range of files, depending on the needs of the team working together.

How to Create a Document Library in SharePoint?

Making a new document library in SharePoint is a simple process. This is how you can do it:

- Go to the site where you want to set up the library of documents.

- In the menu, click the "**New**" button and pick "**Document Library**" from the list of apps that appear.
- Click "**Create**" and give your library a name. Your document library will then be made.

You can change your document library by adding columns, setting rights, and adding themes after you've made it. SharePoint has more than just Document Libraries. You can store files in the Picture Library, the Form Library, the Wiki page Library, the Style Library, and so on.

Giving Your Library a Name and Some Details

Assigning a meaningful name to your library is a critical step in ensuring clarity and facilitating easy identification for everyone on the team within the SharePoint site collection. **Follow these steps to provide additional information about the library through a description statement:**

1. **Locate the Library:**
   - Identify the library for which you want to add a description. Ensure that you are within the SharePoint site collection where the library resides.
2. **Access Library Settings:**
   - Click on the gear icon in the Settings menu, typically found in the top-right corner of the SharePoint page. This will open a menu with various options.
3. **Choose Name and Description:**
   - Within the Settings pane, navigate to the option that allows you to edit the library's name and description. Choose a name that accurately reflects the purpose of the library. Additionally, provide a description that offers more information about the content and purpose of the library.

39

4. **Save Changes:**
   - After entering the desired name and description, click the "Save" button to apply the changes. This ensures that the library is now identifiable with a clear name and is accompanied by additional information for context.

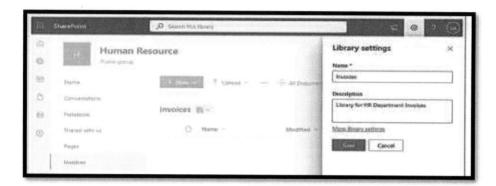

Managing Document Library Settings

To better organize your library and the files in it, you can give each file characteristics and metadata:

1. Find the library whose features you want to change.
2. To change settings, go to **"Settings" > "Library settings" > "More Library settings."**
3. Set up the parameters like name, description, and any extra parameters you've put on the document library settings page.
4. To use the changes, click **"Save."**

You can build and handle a SharePoint Document Library well by following these steps. This will give your team a place to store their files that are well-organized and easy to get to.

Exporting SharePoint Document Library

When handling a document library in SharePoint, the ability to share and download the library is invaluable. Users can conveniently download a copy of the document library for offline storage. **Follow these steps to export and download files:**

1. **Access Document Library:**
   - In the menu, navigate to your document library within SharePoint. Click on the "Library" tab to access library-specific options.
2. **Open with Explorer:**
   - Select the "Open with Explorer" option from the menu. This will initiate Windows Explorer and open the document library, providing a familiar file management interface.
3. **Choose Files and Folders:**

- Within Windows Explorer, pick out the specific folders and files you intend to share or download from the document library. Highlight the items you want to include in the export.

4. **Move Files:**
   - Once the files and folders are selected, move them to the desired location. This step allows you to organize the exported content in a way that suits your preferences.

5. **Alternative: Download Button:**
   - Alternatively, you can choose specific files and folders directly within the document library. Use the "Download" button on the menu to initiate the download process. This method provides a more straightforward approach to downloading selected items.

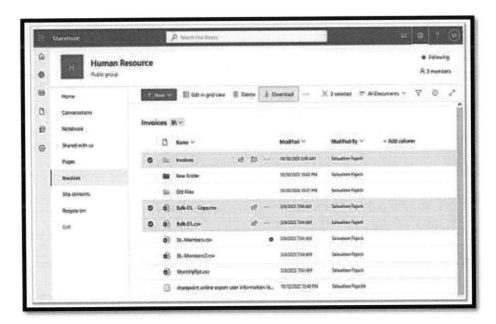

Users have the opportunity to enhance the capabilities of the SharePoint document library system by leveraging its advanced functionalities, leading to improved and seamless collaboration. **To disseminate information from your SharePoint document library, you can proceed with the following steps:**

1. Navigate to the designated SharePoint document library.
2. Opt for the "Export to Excel" feature available in the Library menu.
3. Access the Excel file generated and stores it in your preferred location.

Getting rid of the Document Library in SharePoint

Modifying the name of your SharePoint document library or removing it entirely can be accomplished by adhering to the subsequent instructions:

1. In the menu, navigate to your document library and select the "Library" tab.
2. If the intention is to delete the document library, click on "Library Settings" and subsequently choose "Title, description, and navigation."
3. Execute the steps displayed on the screen to eliminate the document library as desired.

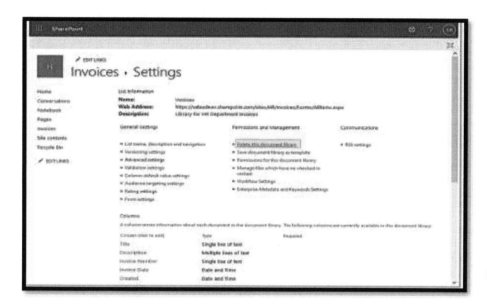

Uploading and Managing Documents

Uploading Files to SharePoint

Uploading files to SharePoint is a simple process that makes it easy to store and share your files. SharePoint makes it easy to share and organize your files, whether you're working on a Word document, an Excel chart, or a PowerPoint show. **Here's what you need to do to add a file to SharePoint:**

- Find the site in SharePoint where you want to add the file.
- Find the "**Upload**" link or button. It's usually near the top of the page.
- To open the file upload box, click on the "**Upload**" button or link.
- In the box that comes up, click "**Browse**" to find the file on your computer that you want to share.
- Click "**Open**" after choosing the file.

- Inside the share box again, you can add more details about the file, like a title or description.
- After you've filled out all the required fields, click the "**Upload**" button to begin the uploading process.
- It might take a while to upload, depending on how big the file is and how fast your internet connection is. You'll see a progress bar that lets you know how the upload is going.
- When the upload is done, you'll see a message or alert letting you know that the file was posted properly.

Viewing and Editing SharePoint Documents

You can easily read and change your papers in your web browser after you've posted them to SharePoint. This gets rid of the need to download things, change them, and then share them again. **These steps will let you see and change a SharePoint document:**

1. Find the paper on the SharePoint site by using the links below.
2. Find the file that you want to read or change.
3. To open the file in the browser, click on the file's name or image.
4. The document will open in the program that comes with that file type by default. For instance, Word files will open in **Word Online** and Excel files will open in Excel Online.
5. Changes can be made to the text, style, or layout of the file once it is opened, just like in a desktop app.
6. You don't have to save the text by hand because SharePoint saves your changes automatically as you work.
7. SharePoint will show you who else is working on the document and highlight their changes in real-time if more than one person is changing it at the same time.

Co-authoring and Collaboration Features

Co-authoring Documents in SharePoint

Document collaboration in SharePoint is enhanced by co-authoring papers. Multi-users can work on the same page at the same time, which makes it perfect for projects that need input and collaboration from many people in real-time. By co-authoring, you can stop sending emails with different copies of a paper back and forth. **These steps will show you how to co-author a doc in SharePoint:**

1. Open the file that everyone wants to work on together.
2. In the upper right part of the screen, click the "**Edit**" button.
3. If someone else is changing the file at the same time, SharePoint will let you know right away.
4. It will save your changes right away after you make them.
5. As other people make changes, you can see them, and SharePoint will join them automatically.

6. You can also use the built-in chat tool to talk to your team members if you need to.

The collaboration process in SharePoint is streamlined by allowing multiple users to co-author papers. It gets rid of problems with version control and makes sure that everyone is, both actually and metaphorically, on the same page.

Collaborating on SharePoint

Collaboration is a key part of any company that wants to be successful. SharePoint is a powerful tool that allows smooth collaboration among team members, allowing them to work together effectively and quickly. Sharing documents and files, co-authoring documents, and using SharePoint discussion boards are three of SharePoint's most important collaboration features, which we will examine in this part.

Sharing Documents and Folders in SharePoint

It's easy to share files and groups in SharePoint. It makes it easy to give entry to certain people or groups, making sure that the right people can see the right information at the right level. By sharing files and papers, you can work together with clients, partners, or coworkers from anywhere. **These easy steps will show you how to share a SharePoint file or folder:**

1. Find the file or folder that you want to share.
2. In the upper right part of the screen, click the **"Share"** button.
3. For each person you want to share the file or folder with, type their email address into the sharing text box.
4. Each person should have the right amount of permission, such as **"View Only," "Edit,"** or **"Full Control."**
5. You can add a message if you want to give more information or directions.
6. To send the file or folder, click the **"Send"** button.

You can easily work together with other people by sharing papers and files in SharePoint if you follow these steps. With this feature, everyone can see the most up-to-date version of the papers, which makes it easier to work together and keep things consistent.

CHAPTER 3
WORKING WITH LISTS AND LIBRARIES

Introduction to Lists and Libraries

Lists vs. Libraries: Understanding the Difference

Lists and libraries may be two of the most used parts of SharePoint. A lot of SharePoint users will already know what these words mean. But do you know what they can do and how they can help you get things done faster? We will talk about SharePoint Lists and libraries in great detail here.

What is a SharePoint list?

A SharePoint list is a group of files that everyone in your company can access and share. It can also be used in different computer parts. Like an Excel chart, it has rows and sections. You can get the information for your list from Excel. Calendars, contact lists, and job lists are all types of lists in SharePoint. But SharePoint groups can be used in a lot more ways. You can start from scratch when making a SharePoint list or a data source. **That or you can pick one of the list themes Microsoft gives you:**

You can add or remove columns and send files to a list after you've made it. The usual view can be changed so that the information is shown the way you want it to be. This makes it much easier to organize the information. You and your coworkers can work well together even if you're not in the same room. You can also easily get to SharePoint groups on any device. They make the process very quick and attentive. And it's never been easier to make a PowerApp from a list if you want to automate your work.

What is a SharePoint Library?

Document libraries are another name for SharePoint libraries. People store files and different types of papers in document libraries. You can handle and organize your info, which is what the name "library" means. You can easily keep track of changes when you are working with your team by using versioning. The details are the most important part of SharePoint folders. Metadata are extra pieces of information about your files. The important information about a document will be shown to you when you add it to a SharePoint library. This tells you when and who posted it. You can make this longer by adding any information that you think is important. It's the same process as adding fields to a list in SharePoint. You can change metadata at any time, even on files that are already open. Lists in SharePoint can even be used to get metadata. You don't have to add the same information over and over again every time you share a new document. You can arrange your info in SharePoint files in any way you like. But we suggest that you use certain rights. That way, everyone can get in; otherwise, things might get complicated.

What's the difference between Libraries and Lists in SharePoint?

- **Collaboration**. You can directly change things in SharePoint Lists. With SharePoint Libraries, you can compare different versions of a file and check them in and out. This makes it easy to keep track of changes.
- **Search results**. Word, PDF, and other files kept in SharePoint Lists will not appear in Search Results. You can't find them because they are just files. In SharePoint Libraries, the main papers will always be shown.
- **Versioning**. The only difference between SharePoint Lists and Libraries is that Lists only have major versions.

Take note: SharePoint Lists and Libraries are very helpful, but they do have some limits. They aren't very flexible, so you might not be able to make all the changes you want. This includes making your menu, and changing who can see certain things and other things. The good news is that each one can hold up to 30 million things. Don't do that, though, because you don't want to be stuck on "ever-loading"!

Creating and Customizing Lists

Creating a List

1. Go to the SharePoint site where you want to make the list.
2. Click "New" and select "**List**" from the available options.

- Pick the kind of list you want to make.

You can change your list by adding columns, items, and information to the list page after you've made it. Make changes to your SharePoint List based on your requirements to make sure your data is properly grouped and shown. You can make changes to your SharePoint List settings as easily or as hard as you want. You can start by changing column types, adding or removing columns, and setting up views. You can also add things to your list by clicking **"New"** and filling in the information for each area before adding the item. Giving you full control over your data's structure, site contents, and layout by starting with a new list lets you make a custom SharePoint List that fits your needs.

Creating a SharePoint List from a Template

Templates for SharePoint Lists make it easy to start making lists because they already have sections and settings that are set up for different uses. **Microsoft has many models to choose from, including**

- Asset Manager
- Content Scheduler
- Event Itinerary
- Issues Tracker
- Recruitment Tracker
- Work Progress Tracker

Utilizing data from a Microsoft Excel file to create either a SharePoint List or an Excel table is a viable option. However, efficient management of these lists necessitates a well-organized site information page. If the decision is made to generate a customized list template, adaptability is key. This involves the ability to modify the template according to specific requirements by adding or removing columns, altering column types, and configuring views, rules, and processes. The utilization of list templates not only saves time and effort but also allows for the exploitation of SharePoint Lists' customization features. Creating a SharePoint List swiftly and effortlessly can be achieved by leveraging pre-existing examples, eliminating the need to initiate the process from scratch. This approach ensures a more streamlined and efficient list creation process. **From a template, you can make a SharePoint List like this:**

1. Open your SharePoint site and go to the page that lists all the pages on it.
2. Click the button that says "**Add an App**."
3. Get the List option and click on any template that's already there.
4. Pick a design that is already made and fits the needs of your List.
5. Make any changes you need to the List.
6. When you're done, click "**Save**."

SharePoint List Management

Effectively managing SharePoint Lists involves tailoring lists to align with the specific requirements of your business. This includes the processes of creation, configuration, and modification to ensure optimal functionality. Additionally, a crucial aspect of list management entails establishing rights and access controls to safeguard data privacy and enhance security measures. The manipulation of SharePoint Lists can be executed through either the SharePoint web interface or the more intricate SharePoint Designer. The latter provides a platform for altering list forms and processes in more complex manners. Users can also exercise the flexibility to customize their views, presenting data in a specific manner, such as filtering by state or sorting by date. This versatility empowers users to tailor SharePoint Lists according to their unique business needs.

Adding Columns to a List

Adding fields is one of the easiest ways to change how your SharePoint List looks. You can make your fields in SharePoint, or you can pick from a lot of standard field types, like text, choice, date/time, and more. You can get data that is specific to your business needs and make data entry faster by adding custom fields. **Here's how to add a field to a list:**

1. Navigate to the list where you intend to include the column.
2. Click on the "Settings" button and select "List settings."
3. Upon reaching the "Columns" section, choose "Add a column."
4. Select the desired column type and assign it a name.
5. Optionally, configure additional features such as the column style, default number, and description to meet your specific requirements.

By clicking the **"Add Column"** link in the list view of modern lists, you can add a new column to the list.

Deleting Columns in a SharePoint List

In the list settings, pick out the column you want to get rid of and click the **"Delete"** button. It's that easy. Remember that removing a column will get rid of all the data that is in that column.

Inserting, editing, and deleting items in a SharePoint list

Items, which are rows of data, are used to store data in SharePoint lists. To handle the data, users can add to, change, or remove things from a list. Adding things to a SharePoint list is one of the most basic ways to manage and organize web data in SharePoint. This method is easy to use, and users of any level of SharePoint skill can learn it quickly. **Here's how to add things to a SharePoint list, step by step:**

Inserting Items

1. Navigate to your SharePoint server or SharePoint Online site and locate the list where you wish to add the item. Open the list.

2. Look for the control on the menu and select "Add new item" to initiate the addition of a new item.

3. The form will appear, presenting various fields corresponding to the columns you configured in your list. These fields may include text boxes, date pickers, dropdown lists, buttons, and other types.

4. Populate each field with the accurate information. For instance, in a task list, you might input details such as the name, summary, due date, and the person responsible for the task. Click "Save" to append the item to the list. Attach files if required.
5. Columns like ID, Created, and Modified will automatically be populated.
6. Validation rules can be implemented to restrict entries or mandate specific forms, ensuring data accuracy and adherence to predefined criteria.

Editing Items

- Open an existing item in the list view and pick "**Edit Item**". The item form view will then open with the current values for that item already loaded.
- You can then make any changes you want to text, numbers, dates, and other fields that can be changed.
- Click "**Save**" to save the changes to the database.
- Versions and past can show earlier numbers and keep track of changes.
- Additionally, you can change multiple list items at once in the Grid view.

Getting Rid of Items

1. Utilize checkboxes positioned next to items to choose multiple entries simultaneously.
2. After selecting one or more items, click "Delete."
3. Alternatively, you can employ the "Delete Item" menu option to eliminate an open item.
4. It's crucial to note that once items are deleted, retrieval is not possible unless restored from backups. Exercise caution to avoid unintended permanent removal of data.

These are the most basic things you can do to manage individual items in SharePoint lists. Learning how to enter, change, and delete data lets you keep your business data up to date in a variety of ways.

Adding Attachments to a SharePoint List

Users can add files to list things in SharePoint Lists, which gives users more information and supporting documents. Follow these steps to add files to a SharePoint List:

1. Navigate to the specific SharePoint List where you intend to incorporate files.
2. Select the desired list item to which you want to attach files.
3. Access the list item menu and click on the "Attachments" button to open the attachments box.
4. Within the list of files, click "Attach File."
5. Choose the file you wish to attach from your device and click "OK."
6. If you need to add more attachments, repeat steps 4 and 5.
7. To save the attached files, click "OK" when you have added all the desired attachments.

Customize SharePoint List Views

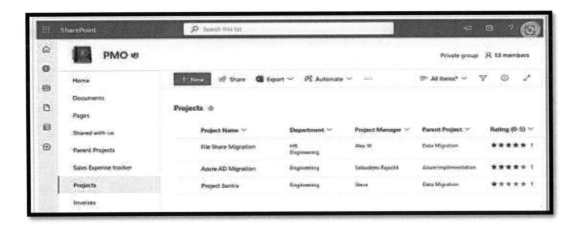

Sorting and Filtering

1. **Sorting:**
   - Sorting allows you to arrange items in a list based on a specific field, such as date, alphabetical order, or status.
   - To sort, choose the column title by which you want to sort and click on it.
   - A single click sorts items in ascending order, and a double click sorts them in descending order.
   - Alternatively, click on the filter icon next to the column header to sort the SharePoint List by a specific property.

51

2. **Filtering:**
   - Filtering enables you to view items that meet specific conditions, such as those created in the last week or assigned to a particular person.
   - Click on the filter icon next to the column header to access filter options.
   - Various filter options are available, including text filters, date filters, and number filters.
   - Utilize these filters to refine the display of information based on your specific criteria.

Grouping

You can put items in a SharePoint List into groups based on a field, like category or department. This can help you see your data in a more organized and useful way. Click on the column header you want to group by and choose "***Group By This Field***" from the menu that comes up.

Creating Custom Views

Customizing views in a SharePoint List to display only the necessary data is a flexible feature, especially when standard views fall short of your requirements. **Here's how you can create a personalized view:**

1. Click on the gear icon located in the upper right corner of the list page.
2. Select "List Settings" to access the settings for the list.
3. Choose "Create View" and follow the provided instructions to set up your customized view.
4. During this process, you can determine which columns to display, configure sorting and filtering options, and assign a name to your view according to your preferences.

In SharePoint, you have the ability to alter how a list or library is presented, ensuring that it showcases information that holds significance for you. This involves adding, removing, and rearranging columns, sorting and filtering data, and creating views that align with your specific needs and preferences.

Conditional Formatting in List Views

Utilizing conditional formatting in SharePoint List views allows you to apply different styles, classes, or icons to fields based on their values, enhancing visual emphasis on specific data under certain conditions. **Here's how you can implement custom views and conditional formatting:**

1. Navigate to the list's column settings.
2. Choose the "Format this column" option.
3. From the "Format column" menu, select "Conditional formatting."
4. Adjust the style settings and manage the rules to achieve the desired visual outcomes.

By incorporating views and conditional formatting when presenting data in your SharePoint Lists, you not only make information visually appealing but also facilitate easier comprehension and analysis on a data-centric platform. This approach contributes to a more user-friendly and insightful data representation.

Managing SharePoint List Permissions

Effectively managing SharePoint List permissions is a crucial aspect of maintaining data privacy and ensuring the security of your company's sensitive information. SharePoint List permissions dictate the level of access individuals or groups have regarding the viewing and modification of the list and its items. Implementing the appropriate permissions ensures that only authorized individuals have the ability to view, edit, or delete data within the list. This is fundamental to safeguarding sensitive information and maintaining the integrity and confidentiality of your company's data.

Understanding SharePoint List Permission Levels

SharePoint List offers predefined permission levels that enable you to control who can access and interact with the list. Here are the standard permission levels:

1. **Full Control:**
   - Users with Full Control permissions possess the authority to perform any action, including managing permissions, deleting the list, and modifying its structure and settings.
2. **Edit:**
   - Users assigned the "edit" permission can add, modify, or remove items from the list. Additionally, they have the capability to alter the list's layout and settings.
3. **Read:**
   - Users holding Read permission can view the list but are restricted from making any modifications or deletions.

SharePoint List comprises three default groups with varying permission levels:
- **Owners:**
  - The Owners group is endowed with Full Control by default, empowering them to modify the list's permissions.
- **Members:**
  - The Members group, having edit permissions by default, can make changes to items within the list.
- **Visitors:**
  - Members of the Visitors group possess read permissions by default, enabling them to view the contents of the list without the ability to make alterations.

Granting and Revoking SharePoint List Permissions

To configure list permissions in SharePoint, follow these steps:

1. **Open the list settings**: Go to the SharePoint site and open the list you want to see. The "**Settings**" gear button is in the upper right corner. Click on it and then choose "**List settings**" from the menu that appears.
2. **Select "Permissions for this list"**: Scroll down to "**Permissions and Management**" on the list settings page and click on the "Permissions for this list" link.
3. **Take care of permissions**: SharePoint will show you the list permissions page, where you can change the permissions for specific people or groups. You can give people or groups permission, choose what amount of permission they have (read, contribute, or full power), and set any other conditions or limits.

Metadata and Content Types

Introduction to Metadata in SharePoint

An Introduction to Metadata in SharePoint: Metadata is extra information about the content of a file, which can be a video, audio file, picture, slideshow, spreadsheet, process map, email, document, webpage, list item, or any other type of file. Metadata, which is also known as "**data about data" or "information about information,"** sorts and describes files in a way that makes them easier to find and move around in your SharePoint sites.

Metadata can be roughly broken down into two categories:

1. Administrative metadata that helps systems and users understand the file better, like the version number, created date, created by, created date, created by, and last changed date.
2. Metadata that tells people about a file and helps them find it, like Location, Department, Topic, Activity, Subject, and Information Type. This usually has to do with what your company knows.

To find the right information, you can use both to help you sort, filter, and improve your navigation and search. Different kinds of metadata can be used together and in new ways to help people find material better. In other words, it doesn't matter how someone searches for something; they can easily get to or find it. One way to cut down their search for an apartment to rent is to start with where they want to live and then add in things like the number of rooms, bathrooms, and gardens that they might want. They could also look for all flats with gardens and then narrow down their options. It is easier to do this if the apartment description has uniform metadata saved on it.

What is managed metadata?

Managed metadata makes sure that all of your SharePoint sites use metadata in the same way. To help your people find the right information at the right time, you can use an organizational language that makes sense to them. SharePoint lets you handle this from one place using a common classification. After that, new information can be added to the category so that it changes as the business does. It is official when taxonomy divides information into logical groups. These groups can be multi-layered, with main categories and subcategories. The SharePoint Term Store Management tool lets you make and handle term sets, which are made up of the information terms you've set up (this is what links multiple categories and subcategories possible).

SharePoint Term Store - term set Department example

Term Store - term set options for managing terms

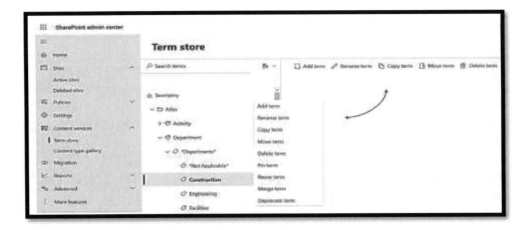

Term Store - term set management options

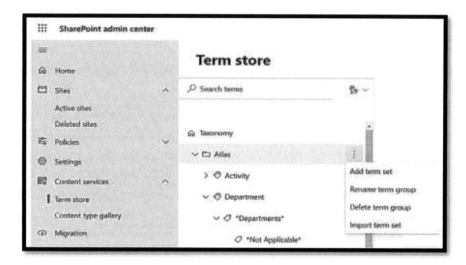

Best practice metadata management leads to:

- When metadata management is done right, users can order their files in more useful and appealing ways.
- Quickly sort, filter, and group files.
- Searches are faster because search engines are geared toward making results more relevant when they have clear information.
- File references that are the same across your SharePoint account, so you can work with them in the same way.

Why use metadata instead of folders

When you compare information and files on an enterprise-wide level, you can see the major difference. You should use folders. They are clear and easy for everyone to use. Folders are back with the release of MS Teams. Each channel formed in an MS Teams site now has its folder to store files under the usual SharePoint Document Library.

However, folders do have limitations:

- You need to know how groups are organized to move through them. Most of the time, only the person who made it can understand it.
- Not always used the same way, and when folder template designs are required, they are often changed to fit individual needs.
- Files can be linked to more than one folder, which can lead to people putting the same file in multiple folders, which makes duplicate files.
- Folders don't make it easier to navigate, sort, or search.

Metadata is great because it solves these problems and more when groups don't work. Should you not care about folders at all? Most likely not. They are used to manage channels in MS Teams sites, as was already mentioned, and they can be useful if you have a group of files that need specific permissions applied so that only certain members of the site can view them. When managing this type of use, folders are very helpful, and if information is used, the two can easily work together to get the most out of both, as explained below.

Why manage metadata?

A lot of the time, information in SharePoint is not handled. If users are allowed to, they can add their values at the SharePoint site level. However, this makes the values too broad, hard to control, and unpredictable. If you don't handle your information, it could get harder to find things and move around in all of your SharePoint sites. Say you use "**HR**" in some places and "**Human Resources**" in others. This means that the search term you use will affect the results you get. Such words and sentences can be taught or set up to understand each other, and they can also be handled as synonyms in the SharePoint Term Store. For more complicated uses, both of these ways can be used, but they need to be checked and validated all the time. Managed metadata takes care of this all at once. Of course, it's even better to use all three at the same time.

Inconsistent metadata and non-organizational language at a site level leads to:

- Increased time to find anything
- Longer time for new joiners to get up to speed
- Greater likelihood of information silos and duplication of files
- Greater likelihood of having to ask others for help finding files
- Greater likelihood of people creating their collections

Groups can decide what values to use by making rules and setting up control practices. "**Metadata owners**" are sometimes in charge of this. These are the people who create, update, and organize the metadata. But everyone is still expected to follow the rules set by the group. Coordinating and agreeing on accuracy can take a lot of time, and it can be hard to put everything into practice site by site. There are other ways to make it easy to create and handle metadata, which will make the whole user experience better for everyone. There must be a better way to handle information. There is, of course. Letting the system do the information work for you will save you time and stress. Keep reading.

How to make applying metadata easier for everyone

Many of the problems listed above can be fixed with auto-tagging tools. They automatically create information, so the end user doesn't have to do much or anything at all. By using these tools, you can make sure that all of your SharePoint sites are consistent and that new content is added with the right information.

This step is automated so that no one has to think about how to tag a file. This is when the company sees the real value of managed metadata. **Several approaches are available and can be combined:**

- Using a tool like ClearPeople's Atlas, add your Information Architecture (controlled information) to the design of your site.
- Taxonomy ontology tools to keep track of your agreed-upon information architecture and then apply it to every file.
- Tools for machine learning and artificial intelligence (AI), like Microsoft SharePoint Syntex and Viva Topics, suggest information based on trends that have already been learned and taught. These tools can be used before or after a file is created.

Making metadata a part of your site design is the best way to get it to work in SharePoint. You can take your controlled metadata to the next level by adding machine-learned and taught metadata on top of this. You can get help from Atlas, Viva Topics, and Syntex all at the same time. Atlas starts you off on the path to organizationally managed information by letting you apply the agreed-upon terms regularly when creating a site and making changes as needed. This experience is improved by Viva Topics, which suggests topics and finds connections between material, interactions, and people's knowledge. When metadata is made automatically during the content editing stage, Syntex can be used to improve the quality of each file's metadata based on rule sets that have already been set up. Atlas makes it easier and faster for people to use SharePoint metadata by adding metadata to files automatically based on where they are saved. This lets people find the file from anywhere they look. This metadata can be added to and changed centrally to adapt to changes in the company. Viva Topics uses the selected information that Atlas applies along with new content to make your content easier to find and connect with other content. People don't have to do extra tagging by hand when SharePoint Syntex improves the quality and accuracy of information at the file level.

In short, it doesn't have to be hard to make, handle, or use SharePoint information; just remember these tips:

- Don't make things too complicated; start small and make changes as you go.
- Don't make up words just for the fun of it.
- Don't make your employees tag files; instead, let where they save the file decide most of the information.
- Use your organization's metadata in one place and on all of your sites.
- Think about what terms need to be the same and where some room for interpretation is needed.
- Use sensible structures (**category -> subcategory**) when they make sense, and try to keep them to three or four levels at most.

You should think about what people want and how they will want to find, identify, travel, or look. The truth is that they will use a mix of these methods, so whatever you do must work for everyone.

Creating and Using Content Types for Document Management

Step 1: Determine the types of documents you want to store in your SharePoint DMS

Putting all of your business's files in one SharePoint Document Library is not a good idea. With SharePoint DMS, the main goal is to group papers that are somewhat connected and have the same protection and permissions. **As an example of this type of SharePoint DMS, let's say you want to store different financial papers, such as:**

- Invoices
- Purchase Orders
- Quotes
- Estimates
- Receipts

Not in the same document library or DMS if you want to store papers that belong to different sections and have different users, permissions, and security. You should instead divide them into several sites or libraries.

Step 2: Categorize Documents for Your SharePoint Document Management System

When establishing a SharePoint Document Management System (DMS) to safeguard financial documents, it's essential to define distinct categories for efficient organization.

In this scenario, let's outline the types of documents we aim to store:

1. **Purchase Orders:**
   - Documents related to the formal request for goods or services, specifying the type, quantity, and agreed-upon terms.
2. **Invoices:**
   - Records detailing the amount owed for goods or services provided, typically including itemized charges, payment terms, and relevant details.
3. **Receipts:**
   - Documents serving as evidence of financial transactions, acknowledging the acceptance of funds, goods, or services.

Step 3: Define metadata for each of the categories above

Most likely, each of the above groups will have its own set of information. Like, you could tag all Purchase Orders with the PO number, the vendor's name, and the date of the PO. Bills can be marked with the Invoice Number, the Client Name, the Date Received, and the Date Paid. Lastly, receipts can be labeled with the name of the vendor, the date they were issued, a description, and the name of the employee who issued the receipt. In this case, it might look like this:

Purchase Order
- PO #
- Vendor
- PO Date

Invoice
- Invoice #
- Client
- Date Received
- Date Paid

Receipt
- Vendor
- Receipt Date
- Description
- Employee

Step 4: For each metadata property, define the type of that property/column

Like a date, an option/drop-down menu, or a free text field. That is what we will need when we make our columns in the next step.

Step 5: Create your metadata columns

- You can make your column at the library level, but making columns at the site level is always the best way to do it. You can then use your articles on other sites and libraries. For us, building our information sections at the Site level will also let us make global content types in the future.

- Click on the Site Gear icon, then go to **Site Settings > Site Columns** (under Web Designer Galleries), and finally click on **Add Column**.
- Use the information we got in Step 3 to make your notes column. I will make a seller Column, which will have a drop-down menu of all the seller names, as a sample.

- Do the steps above again for each column you found.

Step 6: Create Content Types

- Go to the Site Collection's root (or the site where you made all of your site columns in Step 5).
- **Site Settings > Site Content types**.
- Click on "Create link"

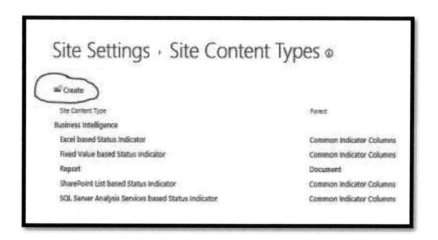

- On the following screen, assign a name to your Content-Type, such as "Purchase Order." Provide a brief description outlining the characteristics and purpose of this Content-Type. In the middle of the page, find two drop-down menus.
- Choose "Document Content Types" from the first menu and then select "Document" from the second menu. This configuration informs SharePoint that the Content-Type will be managing documents within a Document Library.
- In the Group section at the bottom of the screen, select how you want to group your Content Types. You can use the default "Custom group" or create your own custom group, similar to Site Columns. Press the OK button to confirm and save the settings for your Purchase Order Content-Type.

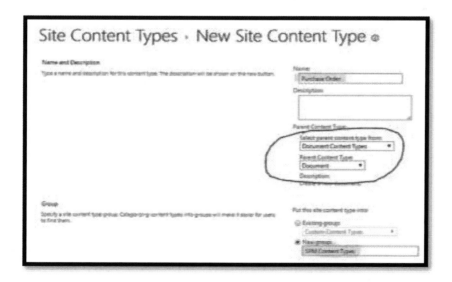

- On the subsequent screen, resembling the illustration provided, you will encounter the display of our next steps. At this point, our objective is to establish a connection between the recently created Content Type, essentially a category, and the associated custom metadata, represented by columns. While there exists the flexibility to modify various aspects of content types, our current focus will be on the integration with site sections. To initiate this process, select the option "Add from existing Site Columns." Direct your attention to the pre-existing Title Column for reference. Subsequently, we will incorporate the newly generated columns we have formulated.

- Your next screen will look like the one below. Choose the group you used to order all of your site's columns (i.e. **Custom Columns**) from the drop-down menu next to "**Select columns from**". This will narrow down the list of site fields to only those that belong to that group. From the list of **Available Columns**, pick the site columns that go with the chosen **Content Type**. Then, use the "**Add**" button to add them to the right side of the selection screen. For us, these are the PO number, the vendor's name, and the PO date. At the bottom of the screen, click OK.

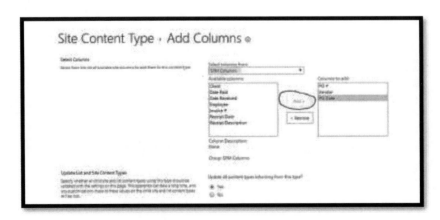

63

- The result should be the page below, where the unique sections have been added to the Content-Type.
- That's all for the first type of material. Do the first seven steps again for each of the other material types.

Step 7: Establish a Document Library on the designated site for your SharePoint Document Management System (DMS)

Assuming familiarity with the process of creating a new site and adding a Document Library, refrain from utilizing the default document library. Instead, follow these guidelines:

Step 8: Prepare the Document Library for Custom Content Types and Custom Metadata

In order to ready our Document Library for the incorporation of "metadata" prior to introducing site content types, certain intricate adjustments are necessary. **Here's a step-by-step breakdown:**

- Navigate to the Library Tab and access Library Settings to unveil all the "administrative" configurations.
- Select Advanced Settings.
- Opt for "Yes" under Allow management of content types to enable the integration of our designated types of site information into the document library.
- Shift focus to the middle of the screen and select the "No" radio button adjacent to "Make 'New Folder' command available???" to discourage the creation of folders when the library utilizes information, ensuring a clear demarcation between the two entities.
- Confirm the changes by clicking the OK button located at the bottom of the page.
- Return to the Library Settings page and proceed to Versioning Settings.
- Verify that the option to "Create major versions" is selected, ensuring the appropriate configuration for versioning settings.

Step 9: Add custom content types to the document library

Now we're getting to the fun stuff. We can now add the special content types we made in Step 6 to our document library. To do this:

- Find the middle of the Library Settings Page and scroll down. You will find a part called **"Content-Type"** there. This is the part of a document library that shows up after we turn on content types in the last step. There is only one Content Type shown by default, which is called **Document**. In the end, we will get rid of it. But let's add our material types first. Click on **Add from existing site content types**

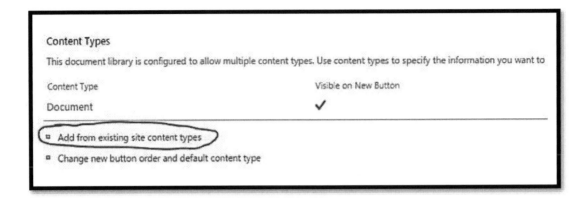

- Select the distinct content types you crafted on the subsequent screen. Utilize the drop-down menu to opt for the grouping employed to organize your Content Types, mirroring the approach taken with site sections. Identify and select the custom content types, subsequently clicking the "Add" button to transfer them to the right side of the screen. Finalize the process by pressing the OK button.

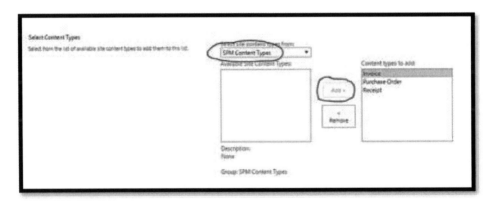

- The main part of your page will look like this, with special content types added next to the document type that was set as the default.

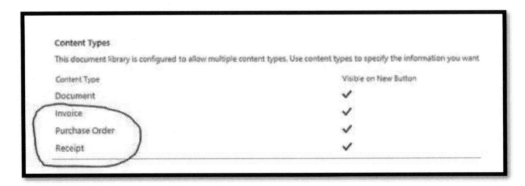

- Observably, upon closer inspection, it becomes apparent that not only were the document types successfully incorporated, but also all the corresponding site sections seamlessly transitioned. These can be readily observed at the bottom of the screen within the Columns column. This section not only displays the added columns but also provides insights into their utilization, showcasing the types of information they encapsulate. This cohesive integration stands as a testament to the robust functionality of the system.

- Let's get rid of that basic content type now that we don't need it in our SharePoint DMS. To do that, go to the Content Types area (middle of the screen) and click on Document Content Type. Then, click on **Delete this content type.** A message will tell you not to do that. Press **OK.**
- Hide the **Title Field** is an additional option, but I prefer to do it. Every content type comes with a **Title Field** by default. It can sometimes mean that the user has to make an extra note. I like to keep it secret. To hide it, go to the content type, click on the **Title Column**, and select the Hidden radio button. Do this again for every other content type.

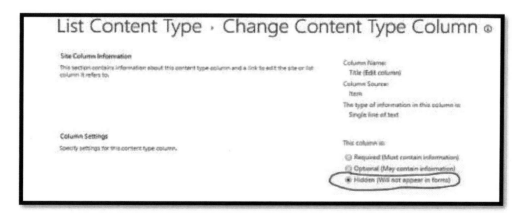

Step 10: Implement Metadata Navigation

As we approach the final stages of configuring our SharePoint Document Management System (DMS), we have a couple more steps to undertake. A feature that I find particularly valuable in any SharePoint list or document library is Metadata Navigation. This feature becomes especially relevant when dealing with information-centric environments. It equips users with visually appealing tools to efficiently search for files, documents, or items within the list or library. To draw a parallel, envision the experience of shopping on Amazon.com, where filters on the left dynamically alter the displayed results on the main page.

Step 11: Optimize SharePoint DMS for a 5,000 Item Limit

Considering the intention to house a substantial number of files within your SharePoint DMS, it is imperative to optimize the document library to accommodate a significant volume. To achieve this in SharePoint, it is crucial to ensure that the document library is configured appropriately, aligning with best practices to mitigate potential challenges associated with the 5,000 item limit. This proactive approach sets the stage for seamless management and accessibility of a large volume of files within the SharePoint DMS.

Step 12: Upload some documents

We're almost there. Go ahead and upload a file now. You will see that there is a Content-Type drop-down and "regular" information values as well. As you move your mouse over the drop-down menu, your information options will change to match. Views below show the change

Step 13: Enjoy your Document Management System in SharePoint!

There you have it! Now that everything is set up, you will have a great SharePoint DMS and a great time using it.

CHAPTER 4

PERMISSIONS AND SECURITY IN SHAREPOINT

Managing SharePoint Online Security: A Team Effort

Tenant settings

Before you even let the people into SharePoint, this is where you should start. But, sadly, most of the time, people start using the platform with the basic settings still in place. You should pay attention to a few renter settings, though. The sharing settings are very important. They can have terrible effects and cause data leaks if they are left to their own devices. Let's begin with this scene.

Sharing settings

To get to the tenant-level sharing settings, go to the **SharePoint Admin Center** and click on **Sharing** under Policies. The fact that the scale for SharePoint and OneDrive is at the same level as the word "**Anyone**" should be the first thing that gets your heart racing. Isn't it freaky that people can share folders and files with links that don't require the other person to sign in? ANY recipient would do. You should slide down one level right away unless you're sure you want to keep it that way!

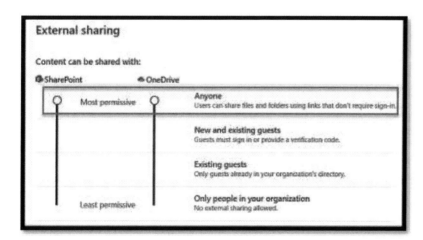

Note: At this point, you don't even need to know the exact OneDrive for Business rules for your business. Not only that, but the scale will also move down one level with the SharePoint setting. Because you can't make it easier for people to share on OneDrive for Business than on SharePoint.

This is how you can choose the right sharing settings between the following once you know what the company policy is:

- New and existing guests
- Existing guests
- Only people in your organization

More external sharing settings

Once more, we have a few options that can help us get a little more if we need to. You can pick any or all of them. But just because you can doesn't mean you should!

- **Limit external sharing by domain**: You can Allow or Block certain sites if this option is chosen. Working together with certain customers or partners is a regular situation. On both the renter level and the site level, you can change this setting.

Note: The other sites will be blocked as soon as you click "**Allow**" on one or more of them. The other names will still be able to connect if you "**Block**" some of them.

Only let people in certain Security Groups share with other people outside the company: If chosen, only people in the private group(s) will be able to share with people outside the group. The sharing settings (tenant) must be set to "**New and Existing Guests**" or "**Anyone**" for this option to be available. Guests must sign in with the same account that was used to send the sharing invitations: As an extra safety measure, this makes sure that the person who is accessing the file(s) is the person you want to be accessing them. If you can, you should choose this option. People who use a verification code need to verify their identity again after [number of days]: A new way has been added where guests will use a one-time PIN to log in for the number of days you set.

Site settings

It's hard to keep your mind off of SharePoint permissions because they are such a big subject. And things don't get better when sites are linked together in groups! Think of the permissions as a peak. The process starts at the top (site level), and as we go down, we can give them to papers one by one.

SharePoint Groups

It doesn't matter if the site is group-connected or not; when you make a site (it depends on the design), three SharePoint groups are automatically made:

- Owners
- Members
- Visitors

There is a permission level for each built-in group. You should use those first, but if they don't work for you, make a new SharePoint group and give it your permission level. You can copy a permission level and choose which options to use or not use depending on your needs.

Best Practice: If you need to, make your own SharePoint group and permission level. Don't change or delete the built-in groups.

Active Directory (AD) Groups

Most businesses already have an Active Directory on-premises that is linked to Microsoft 365. It is suggested that when giving permissions to a SharePoint site, security groups be added to those SharePoint groups. You can make Microsoft 365 security groups right in the admin center, though, and then add them to your SharePoint site as well! SharePoint groups are not the same as Active Directory groups. If you make a SharePoint group, it will only be available on the site where it was made. For easy control, it's best to add security groups to your SharePoint groups. It is possible to add people one at a time to sites, but it will be harder to keep track of them in the future.

Breaking permission inheritance

One time, you might need to let someone use only a library or a document, not the whole site. That is where we can stop permissions from being passed down. This is more of a duty of the Site Owner than of the Site Member. When you make a site and then start building libraries, lists, and sharing documents, all people visiting the site also have access to those libraries and documents. Remember the thing about the crescendo? When removing permission transfer after making the library or list, the usual SharePoint groups (i.e.: Owners, Members, Visitors) will still show under the site permissions settings. Add your account (to keep access), then remove the usual SharePoint groups, and add whoever needs access to this library, which has now unique permissions.

Site Sharing

Sharing on your site will be different if it's not linked to a Microsoft 365 Group. The updated design gives you a better way to manage permissions and gives you more options when sharing.

Sites not connected to Microsoft 365 groups

Things haven't changed much if your site isn't linked to a group. SharePoint experts will still know how to share a site and use the Advanced Permissions Settings, even though the interface is more current.

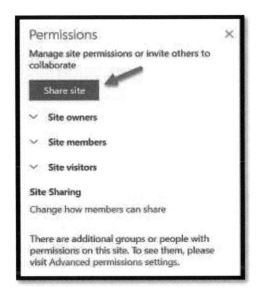

Sites *connected* to Microsoft 365 groups

It is still possible to share the Site only when you have joined a group. In other words, you don't have to share other Microsoft 365 group tools like a shared email, Planner, etc. Then you need to choose **Invite people >> Add members to group** if you want to share the site and include the user(s) in all the tools that come with the Microsoft 365 group. You get to choose!

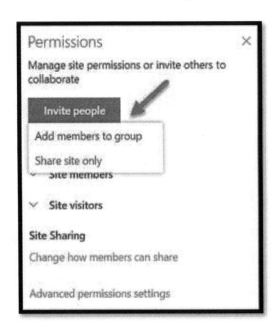

Change how members can share

Having the choice between the following three options is another thing that might make sharing less likely:

- Member-owners and site owners can share files, folders, and the site itself. Shared files and folders can be used by anyone with Edit permissions.
- Members, site owners, and people with Edit permissions can all share files and folders, but only site owners can share the site itself.
- Only people who own the site can share folders, files, and the site itself.

The only difference between the first two bullet points is that in choice 2, only the site owner will be able to share the site. Members won't do it. I had to read it a few times because it was hard for me at first! The third bullet point is pretty clear, but we can see how it might get in the way of people doing their work. What if you need to tell a coworker or customer something? Also, this will make the site owner's job harder... This option could be used if your users are new to SharePoint, if they need more training before they can share with confidence, or if you just don't want them to share at all.

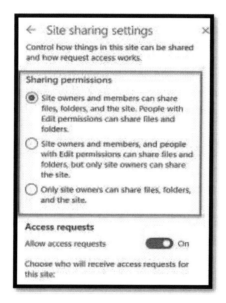

Access Requests

As you can see in the picture above, Access Requests were also turned on by default. What is it? This feature has been around for a while and is better than getting the annoying "*Access denied*" message that you can't do anything about! It's still not fully set up in SharePoint on-premises, but everything is ready to go in SharePoint Online! We only need to decide who should get those requests, write a personalized letter for the person making the request, and view the open requests again.

Two options for who should receive Access Requests:

- Site Owners
- Specific email

Other Security Features to Consider

Multi-Factor Authentication (MFA)

MFA to protect your names is the first thing that comes to mind, and it's not just tied to SharePoint. When we first thought about MFA a few years ago, we were only thinking about applying it to (at least) Global Admins. But in reality, it should be used on all accounts whenever possible.

Security and Compliance

After making SharePoint a safe place to work, we should also make sure that the data that is stored in SharePoint is safe, right? So we'll talk about Sensitivity labels, Retention labels and rules, Data Loss Prevention (DLP), types of sensitive information, and so on. Where are those, though? The *Security and Compliance Center* is in charge of them. As a SharePoint Administrator, should I make and handle those? Most likely not. Someone with access to the Security and Compliance center and the ability to make labels and rules will need to do this. This should ideally be guided by what the company needs, carefully planned, and carried out.

Devices Accessing SharePoint Data

The SharePoint Online Admin Center has more options, but they might need an Azure account.

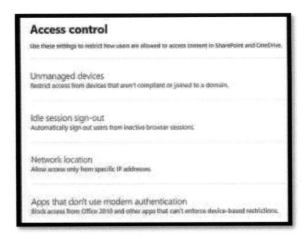

SharePoint Permissions

There are four main types of permissions in SharePoint Online:

1. **Site Permissions:**

Determining who has the visibility and authority to perform actions within a specific SharePoint site, site permissions play a pivotal role. Typically established at the root level of the site, they can also be configured at the subsite level, offering a nuanced control structure.

2. **List Permissions:**

List or library permissions govern the access and modification rights for individuals regarding a particular list or library in a SharePoint site. These permissions can be configured either at the list or library level, allowing for tailored access control.

3. **Folder Permissions:**

In SharePoint Online, the functionality of folder permissions mirrors that of permissions for other elements such as a site or a document library. Users can be allocated varying levels of access to folders, encompassing options like Read, Contribute, or Full Control, ensuring a granular control mechanism.

4. **Item Permissions:**

Dictating who can view and edit a specific item or document within a list or library, item permissions introduce a layer of specificity. Items may possess distinct permissions compared to the overall list, and these permissions can be established at the document or list item level, refining access control.

It is imperative to note that the authority to set permissions for a site or item necessitates being the site owner or possessing the appropriate permissions. In SharePoint Online, permissions are configured at the site level and can cascade down to subsites, lists, libraries, and even specific elements within those lists and libraries. Site administrators hold the responsibility of configuring permissions for a site, and these permissions extend to all associated subsites, lists, and libraries by default unless unique permissions are defined for a subsite, list, library, or item.

SharePoint Permission Levels

In SharePoint Online, the actions an individual or group can undertake within a site, list, library, or item are governed by their assigned permission levels. While certain predefined permission levels, such as Full Control, Edit, and Read, are inherent in SharePoint Online, users also have the flexibility to create custom permission levels if needed.

The default permission levels in SharePoint Online include:

- **Full Control:** Users bestowed with Full Control permissions possess the authority to view, add, modify, and delete any content within the site, list, library, or item. Beyond content manipulation, users with Full Control can manage user permissions, configure item-level security settings, create or remove libraries and lists, customize the site's appearance, and administer site content, library, and list settings.

- **Design:** Those with Design permissions can view and modify content across the site, lists, libraries, or items. Additionally, they have the capability to create and delete lists and libraries. Design-permission users can also influence the visual aspects of the site, altering its look and feel. However, they are restricted from altering security settings for the site, lists, libraries, or items.
- **Edit**: Users with this permission level can view and change any information on the site, list, library, or item. Users who have Edit permissions can't change the security settings for a site, a list, a library, or an item. By default, members of a SharePoint team site have this permission.
- **Contribute**: To get this permission level, users can view and change any content on the site, in a list, a library, or an item. However, they can't make or remove lists or libraries. SharePoint users who only have the "**Contribute**" permissions can't change how the site looks or how it works. They also can't change the security settings for the site, a list, a library, or an item.
- **Read**: Users with this permission level can view material in the site, library, list, or item, but they can't change, add to, or remove anything. Users who only have Read permissions can't change the protection settings for a site, list, library, or item. In most cases, given to site users.
- **View Only**: Users with this permission level can only view material in the site, library, list, or item; they cannot add, change, remove, or edit any of the items. Users with "View Only" permissions can't change the security settings for the site, a list, a library, or an item. They can view pages, set alerts, and view things, but they can't download files to the client apps.

To craft a custom permission level in SharePoint Online, follow these step-by-step instructions:

1. Locate the site where you intend to establish the custom permission level and navigate to its settings page.
2. Proceed to "Settings," then "Site Permissions," and subsequently select "Advanced permissions settings."
3. On the Permissions page, access the "Permission levels" link in the menu.
4. Click on "Add a Permission Level" on the "Permission Levels" page.
5. Provide a name for the new permission level and offer a concise explanation of its intended functionalities.
6. Choose the specific permissions you wish to include in this new level. Options can be selected from a predefined list of permissions such as "Full Control," "Edit," or "Read." Tailor these permissions to align with your specific requirements.
7. To formalize the creation of the new permission level, click the "Create" button.

Once you have successfully crafted the unique permission level, you can allocate it to individuals or security groups as needed, thereby customizing access and control within the SharePoint Online environment based on your organizational needs.

Copy existing Permission Level

If you want to make a new permission level in SharePoint, you can also copy a current permission level. Do the things listed in steps 1 through 3. You can copy any current permission level, like **"Contribute,"** by clicking the **"Copy Permission Level"** button. You can then add or remove permissions like **"Open items"**, **"application pages"**, **"Browse user information"**, **"Personal web parts"**, **"Client integration features"**, **"Remote interfaces"**, and more.

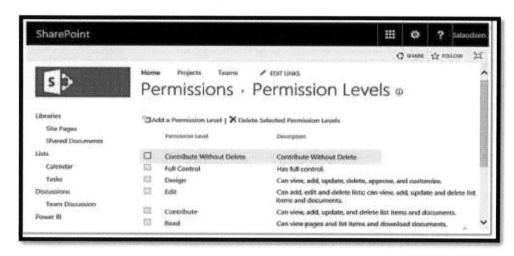

Managing Permissions in SharePoint Online

There are several ways to set and manage permissions in SharePoint Online:

1. **SharePoint Groups**: A SharePoint group is a group of people who all have the same permissions. Different groups can be made for different reasons, like a group for site managers and another group for people who are part of a project team. You can add or remove people from groups whenever you want, and any changes you make to the group's permissions will affect everyone in the group.
2. **Individual Permissions**: On a particular list, library, or item, you can also set permissions for individual people or groups. Any permissions set for a group or level of permission are overridden by permissions set for an individual.

How Do I Manage SharePoint Online Permissions?

In SharePoint Online, the User Interface (UI) serves as the central platform for managing permissions efficiently. Through the UI, users can effortlessly add or remove individuals from their site or document library, assign specific roles and tasks, and organize groups to streamline management of multiple users simultaneously. Distinct levels of permissions are allocated based on the user's role, ensuring that supervisors possess greater control over the site compared to regular users.

Differentiating between Private Team Sites and Public Team Sites adds an additional layer of control. By associating a Microsoft 365 group with a SharePoint site, administrators can dictate the site's privacy setting as either private or public. This decision determines whether only specified users can access the site or if all company users can access it by extending access to the designated group "Everyone except external users" in SharePoint. Furthermore, when initiating a new team site or discussion site in SharePoint Online, foundational SharePoint groups are automatically established. These default groups play a pivotal role in governing who can view the site and its content, as well as defining the associated permissions. This structured approach simplifies the initial setup process while providing a foundation for effective permission management within the SharePoint Online environment.

This is a list of the basic groups and what permissions they have:

1. **The owners**: This group controls the whole site and everything on it. They can change other things about the site, add and remove people, and set permissions.
2. **Members**: This group can make changes to the site, add and remove material, set up lists and libraries, and control permissions for their papers and things.
3. **Visitors**: People in this group can only read what's on the site. Any material on the site can be viewed by them, but not changed.
4. **Approvers**: This group can either accept or reject papers that have been sent to them for review.
5. **Hierarchy Managers**: This group can make sites and pages in the site collection and control them.

Set up a SharePoint Group: You can make your special groups in SharePoint and give them the permissions you need in addition to these basic groups.

Folder level permissions in SharePoint Online

You can indeed restrict access to specific folders within a list or library in SharePoint Online by employing folder-level permissions. **Here's a step-by-step guide on how to set permissions at the folder level:**

1. Navigate to the list or library containing the folder for which you want to modify permissions.
2. Select the desired folder within the list or library.
3. Access the ribbon and click on the "Files" tab. Subsequently, click on the "Manage Access" button.

4. In the "Manage Access" box, you can add individuals or SharePoint security groups and assign them the appropriate permission level. To remove someone from the list, click on the "X" next to their name.

5. After making the necessary changes, click the "Save" button to apply the modified permissions.

It's crucial to note that folder-level permissions in SharePoint Online operate independently of list or library permissions. If you wish to grant an individual or security group access to all files within a list or library, you must provide permissions at the list or library level. This can be achieved by adding the person or group to the list of individuals and groups with permissions on the list or library's "Permissions" page. By implementing these steps, you can effectively control access to specific folders, tailoring permissions based on your unique requirements.

How to grant access to a document in SharePoint?

1. Locate the file or folder for which you want to modify permissions within the list or library.
2. Select the file and click on the "Share" button. This action will open the "Share with Others" box.
3. In the "Invite People" box, enter the email address of the person or group for whom you want to establish permissions.
4. From the "Permission Level" dropdown menu, select the appropriate access level based on your requirements.
5. Optionally, you can include a message in the "Add a message (optional)" box to provide context or additional information.
6. To send the invitation and configure the permissions, click the "Share" button.

It's important to note that to set permissions at the item level, the owner must first break the inheritance of permissions from the parent list or library. Once this is done, the supervisor can add individuals or groups as members of the specific item and allocate distinct permissions. Keep in mind that the available file-level permissions in the "Permission Level" dropdown may vary depending on your organization's SharePoint setup. If you need permissions beyond the choices available in the dropdown, you may need to request additional permissions from a supervisor or someone with the appropriate access rights.

How to check user Permissions in SharePoint Online?

Indeed, regularly reviewing and managing permissions on a SharePoint Online site is crucial, especially in environments with diverse roles and responsibilities. **Here's a step-by-step guide on how to check site permissions in SharePoint Online:**

1. Navigate to the specific SharePoint site for which you want to review permissions.
2. In the top right corner of the page, click on the "Settings" button. From the ensuing menu, select "Site settings."

3. On the "Site Settings" page, locate the "Users and Permissions" section and click on the "Site permissions" link.
4. The "Site permissions" page will display a comprehensive list of all individuals and security groups that have been granted access to the site, accompanied by the respective permission levels assigned to them.

To check permissions on a specific library or list within the site, follow a similar process:

1. In the library or list, click on the name of the list or library itself.
2. This action will bring up a box displaying the exact permissions that have been allocated to the list or library.

It is important to note that to view site, list, or library permissions, you must already possess the requisite permissions. By following these steps, you can efficiently audit and manage permissions within your SharePoint Online environment, ensuring that access is appropriately granted based on organizational needs.

Anonymous Access in SharePoint Online

If your external sharing settings are configured to "Anyone," you can generate a unique link that allows access without the need for passwords. Here's a step-by-step guide:

1. Open SharePoint Online and locate the file or folder you wish to share.
2. Right-click on the item, and then click the "Share" button.
3. In the link settings, choose "Anyone with the link" and input the email addresses of the individuals who should receive the link.
4. From the drop-down box, select the desired permissions for these external users, such as Edit or View.
5. Click "Send" to finalize the sharing process.

This will generate a unique link that you can share with people who are not part of your organization, allowing them to access the specified file or folder without requiring a password. It's important to note that the effectiveness of these steps depends on the external sharing settings configured for your SharePoint Online environment. Always ensure that your sharing settings align with your organization's security policies and requirements.

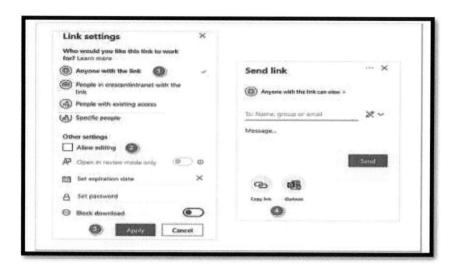

Best Practices for Security and Compliance

Data Loss Prevention (DLP) in SharePoint

Data loss prevention is a set of tools and rules that help businesses keep private data from getting out to people who shouldn't have it. You can keep an eye on and change data that is moving, at rest, or being used with these tools. Data loss protection strategies can find and stop people who aren't supposed to be accessing private data from doing so, as well as stop data from getting out by accident. To stop data loss, businesses must first figure out what private data they need to keep safe. Personal data, banking data, intellectual property, and other types of private data can be included in this. Companies can make rules about how to protect private data once they know what it is.

Microsoft Purview Data Loss Prevention

One way to keep data safe is to use Microsoft Purview, a cloud-based data control tool. Software companies can use Microsoft Purview to make rules about how to keep private info safe. You can use these rules to both watch data in real-time and scan data that is already stored. Many built-in rules in Microsoft Purview can be used to keep private information safe in Microsoft 365 services like Teams, Exchange, SharePoint, and OneDrive. If a group needs them, these rules can be changed to fit their needs. Microsoft Purview has rules to stop data loss and tools for finding data, organizing data, and tracking data history. You can use these tools to find private data, keep track of how it is used, and make sure that data security laws are being followed.

SharePoint and Data Loss Prevention

We know how important it is for our company to keep private information safe in SharePoint. To do this, we've put in place data loss prevention (DLP) rules that let us find, keep an eye on and protect private things across all of our site groups instantly.

SharePoint DLP Policies

SharePoint DLP policies are a list of rules that are used to find private information in SharePoint and keep it safe. You can use PowerShell or the SharePoint admin tool to make and control these rules. To make a SharePoint DLP policy that works, we need to know what the different parts are that make up the policy. Policy rules, policy tips, acts, and exceptions are some of these parts. We can set the conditions for finding and protecting private information by setting these parts.

Sensitive Information in SharePoint

In SharePoint, sensitive information can be anything from cash data to *personally identifiable information (PII).* To keep this information safe, we need to find it and use the right safety steps. Using DLP searches is one way to find private information in SharePoint. Based on conditions that have already been set, these queries can be used to search SharePoint site groups for private data. Once we know it's been found, we can protect the data by blocking access or encrypting it.

Using sensitivity marks is another way to keep private data safe in SharePoint. SharePoint papers and other content can be put into groups based on how sensitive they are by adding sensitivity marks. After this rating, safety steps like encryption or limited access can be put in place.

Creating DLP Policies

Here are the steps we need to take to make a DLP policy in SharePoint:

- Go to the center for managing SharePoint.
- Click on "**Policies**" in the menu on the left.
- Click on "Data **loss prevention**" and then "**Make a policy**."
- Pick what kinds of information you want to keep safe and what you will do if you find any private information.
- Make the policy tips and alerts work.
- Keep the rule.

It's important to remember that DLP policies can be hard to understand, so it's important to plan and get everyone involved to make sure the policy works.

Policy Tips and Alerts

Policy tips and reports are important parts of SharePoint's DLP rules. Policy tips let users know when they're about to share private information, and alerts let managers know when private information has been shared. **These are the steps we need to take to set up policy tips and alerts:**

1. Go to the "**Policies**" tab in the CMS for SharePoint.
2. Go to "**Data loss prevention**" and pick out the policy you want to change.
3. In "Policy tip settings," we can change the message that shows up when a user is about to give out private information.
4. Under "**Alerts**," we can set up an alert to let us know when private data is shared.

It's important to remember that policy tips and alerts can help us spot possible security risks and take action before any data is lost.

Policy Tips

When you work with DLP rules in SharePoint, be sure to remember these policy tips:

- Get people who have a stake in the policy involved in the planning process to make sure it works.
- Make sure the policy is always up-to-date by reviewing and updating it regularly.
- Teach people how to find and handle private information and how important it is to keep data safe.
- Make sure that policy tips are written in clear, short language so that users know the risks of sharing private information.

We can make sure that our DLP rules stop data loss in SharePoint by following these policy tips.

CHAPTER 5

COLLABORATION IN SHAREPOINT

Working with SharePoint Teams and Groups

Groups, SharePoint, and Teams are three important parts of the Microsoft 365 environment that can help you work together and talk to your team more clearly.

- **Group** is a service that lets you gather people, talks, and material in one place. Your team can collaborate on tasks, share files, and have conversations in a shared area you can build for them.
- **SharePoint** lets you store, organize, and share files with your team. It is a web-based tool for collaboration and document management. You can make web pages, document files, and lists that everyone on your team can view from any device.
- **Users** can chat, share files, and work on projects together with their teams in real-time on Teams, a chat-based collaboration tool. Microsoft tools like SharePoint and OneNote work with it, so you can get to all of your files and notes from one place.

A smooth collaboration experience for your team is provided by these three organizations. Teams can be made and tasks can be coordinated with groups. SharePoint can be used to store and organize things that are connected to the team's work. Through Teams, you can chat, share files, and work on projects together at the same time.

In what way do these services work together?

A strong set of collaboration tools that can help your team work better is made up of Groups, SharePoint, and Teams. These services work together in the following ways:

Groups and SharePoint

Groups and SharePoint work well together, and you can use them both to help your team work together better. When you make a Group in SharePoint, it also builds a site that is related to the Group immediately. You can store and organize things that are important to the Group's work on this site. The Group's SharePoint site can be used to add SharePoint document files, lists, and pages, which will make them available to all Group users. Additionally, you can use SharePoint permissions to restrict who can view, edit, and delete files. Version control allows you to keep track of how files have changed over time. You can also connect SharePoint to Microsoft Teams, which lets you get to your SharePoint site right from Teams. In other words, you can share files from SharePoint right in Teams and work on them with your team at the same time.

Teams and Groups

Because Microsoft Teams is built to work well with Groups, you can use Teams to work together with other people in a Group. The option to make a Group goes with creating a new Team. With this, you and your team members will be able to chat, share files, and work on them together in real-time. OneNote, SharePoint, and other Microsoft tools all work with Teams, so you can get to all of your files and notes from one place. When you make a new Channel in Teams, a new folder is added to the SharePoint site for the Group that goes with it. This means that all the files and talks that are connected to that Channel will be kept in that folder. This makes it easy to keep your work organized.

Teams and SharePoint

When you make a new Team, a SharePoint site that is tied to the Team is also made immediately. SharePoint lets you store and organize files that are important to the work of your team, and you can share those files right in Teams. Additionally, you can use SharePoint permissions to restrict who can view, edit, and delete files. Version control allows you to keep track of how files have changed over time. Teams make a new folder in the related SharePoint site when you add a new Channel. This means that all the files and talks that are connected to that Channel will be kept in that folder. This will make it easy to keep your work organized.

Creating and Managing SharePoint Teams

Microsoft Teams is a collaboration tool that lets you chat with other people about a subject or job. You can use it to make and handle SharePoint teams. You can use the tools that are linked to each team to work with other people. If you want to make websites, share material, and store files, SharePoint is the tool for you. A new SharePoint site is made and linked to the new team when you make one from scratch. When you take a current Microsoft 365 group and turn it into a new team, the team is linked to the SharePoint site that is linked to the group. A new team is made and linked to a current SharePoint site when you add Teams to it. To handle settings and permissions when Teams and SharePoint are linked, you can find out more about how to connect Teams and SharePoint, as well as basic terms and structure. You can also tell the difference between SharePoint and Teams and move between them.

Create a Microsoft Team from a SharePoint team site

- Go to a team site that you own that is linked to a group.
- In the bottom left area of your team site's home page, click **"Add real-time chat."** You can also find the **"Add real-time chat"** button in the **"Next Steps"** panel, which you can reach from the top right corner of your team site.
- Click on **"Add real-time chat"** to bring up a screen that tells site owners briefly about the benefits of adding Microsoft Teams to their SharePoint sites.

- To add SharePoint files as tabs in Teams, click **Continue** to view more options. Pick out news posts, lists, document files, and SharePoint pages to add to Microsoft Teams. This will let your team work together in one space. Keep in mind that the team site's usual document library is already chosen and can't be changed. You will be able to find this library in the Teams channel under the Files tab. Your site's home page will also be chosen for you, but you can change your mind. To view the most frequently used tools on your team site, choose from the recommended area.
- Click "**Add Teams**" to make a new Team channel with the tools you chose as tabs.

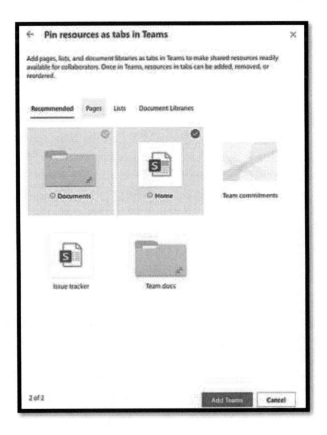

Setting Up Discussion Boards for Team Communication

Step 1: Go to the Microsoft 365 Portal.

- Open your Microsoft 365 account and go to the "**SharePoint**" area.

Step 2: Add an App

- Go to the SharePoint settings and click on "**Add an App.**"

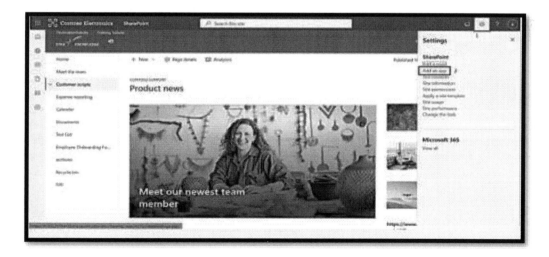

Step 3: Enable Classic Experience

- Pick "**Classic Experience**" to get to the app's settings.

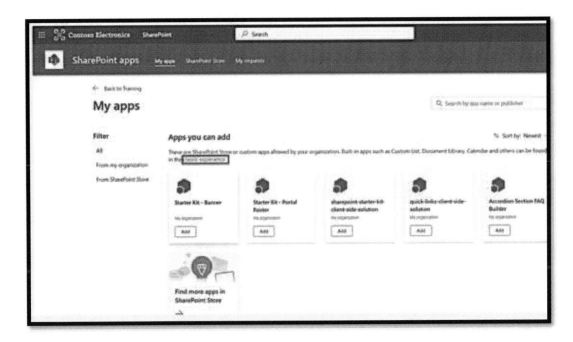

Step 4: Select "Discussion Board"

- Look through the list of apps in the Classic Experience for "Discussion Board" and click on it.

Step 5: Provide Board Details

- There are two options for naming your discussion board: name it and add a statement of what it's for. Once done, click **"Create."**

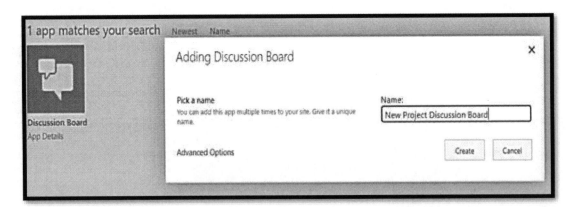

Step 6: Access Your Board

- The discussion board you just made will now show up in the list of apps. To get to it, click on its name.

Step 7: Start a Discussion

- To start a new discussion topic, click **"New."** Type in the subject, write the message, add any important information, and then save your post.

Step 8: Engage in Conversations

- The discussion board for you is now ready to go. You can join or start a chat with other people on your team by clicking on it.

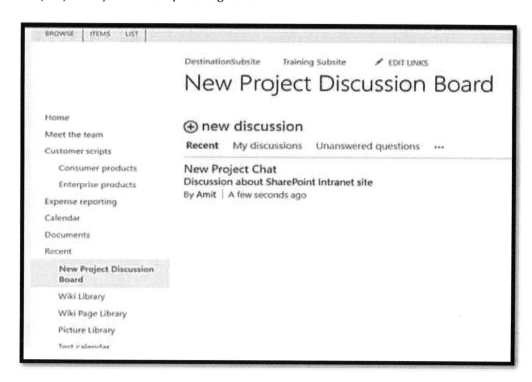

CHAPTER 6
CUSTOMIZING SHAREPOINT SITES
Site Customization Basics

- Change your site's style, title, image, and main menu. To choose from various styles, layouts, and colors, you can use the Change the look option in the site settings. You can also change the links on your site's menu and add your brand.

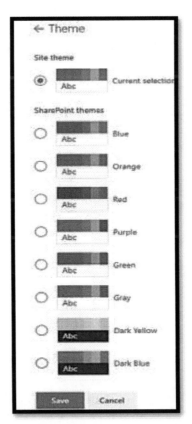

- Make your site look like a template. SharePoint has some site themes that come with pages, news post templates, page templates, and web parts that are already filled out and ready to use. These templates can be changed to fit your needs. For instance, you can use the Event template to let people know about an upcoming event, or the Human Resources template to let workers know about their perks, careers, pay, and the rules of the company.
- Add useful and changing information to your site pages with web parts. Web parts are reused parts that show data or material from different sources. You can add text, pictures,

movies, charts, maps, forms, and more to your site pages with web parts. Web parts can also have their look and behavior changed to fit your needs.

Putting in quick links

Quick links are a great thing about SharePoint. All it takes is one click to get to important information or pages that are often viewed. It's easy to add quick links to SharePoint. It saves time by making quick links to tools that you use often. **They can connect to files, team sites, or websites outside of the team.**

- First, go to the page where you want the link to be. To change something, click "**Edit**." Find a place on the page, like a content area or web part zone.
- After that, click "**+ Add a new web part**." This brings up a list of site parts. Pick out the web part called "**Quick Links**."
- Press the pencil button in the top right corner of the Quick Links web part to make changes. It shows up as a fly-out screen. You can add links and group them.
- Press the "**+ Add Link**" button to add a link. There will be a form where you can put the link's title and URL. You can pick a new tab if you want it to open.
- Do this again for every link. When you're done, click somewhere else to save. Now that you have them, your quick links will be accessible.

Adding Web Parts and Apps

Exploring Out-of-the-Box Web Parts

What are SharePoint web parts?

Web parts are simply things on a page that show information. It's like putting together puzzle parts to make a website page. These web parts are small programs that store and show a certain kind of information (it varies from web part to web part). SharePoint comes with web parts that are already set up. You can use third-party web parts on your site, though, which you can find in Microsoft 365. When you add out-of-the-box web parts to your site pages, they are ready to use and can show different kinds of information and functions. Out-of-the-box computer parts are things like

- **News web part**: This web part lets you show news articles from your site or other sites in different layouts and styles. You can sort the news by date, source, or theme as well.
- **Events web part**: With the help of this web part, you can show future events from your site or other sites in a schedule or list view. You can also connect the events to other calendars or Outlook.
- **Highlighted content web part (HCWP):** This web part lets you show content from your site or other sites on the fly based on things like content type, information, or keywords. You can change how the web part looks and how it works as well.

Add apps for SharePoint-to-SharePoint sites

People who own sites can add SharePoint apps from these places:

- From the list of apps that are already added to a site (basic apps, like standard libraries and lists, and apps that have already been bought).
- From the App Store.
- From the SharePoint store.

Keep in mind that someone who is logged in as a system account can't launch an app. The app asks for permissions it needs to work (like access to Search or the ability to make a list) when you add it to SharePoint. This app won't run if you don't have those permissions. Get the permissions you need from your boss or have someone else with those permissions add the app. Here are the steps you need to take to add apps from these places.

To add an app from a site's list of apps that can be used,

- First, make sure that the user account that is doing this is part of the site Owners group.
- Click **Add lists, libraries, and other apps** on the home page, next to **"Get started with your site."**

You can get started with your site control if it's not on the home page. To do this, click the Settings icon, then **View Site Contents**. Finally, on the **Site Contents** page, click **Add an App**.

- Click the app you want to add to the **"Your Apps"** list.
- If it's a custom component, trust the app by following the steps given. If it's a SharePoint component, name the app.

The SharePoint app has been added and can be found in the **Apps** part of your Site Contents list.

To add an app from an App Store

- First, make sure that the user account that is doing this is part of the site Owners group.
- Click Add lists, libraries, and other apps on the home page, next to "Get started with your site."

You can get started with your site control if it's not on the home page. To do this, click the Settings icon, then View Site Contents. Finally, on the Site Contents page, click Add an App.

- Click on **From Name**.

Name is the name of the App Catalog for your company. "From Contoso" is one example.

Tip: Apps that are marked as **"Featured"** in the App Catalog will also show up in the main list of apps.

- Pick out an app to add.

- If you believe the app, click **Allow Access** in the message that says "**Grant Permission to an App"** dialog box.

The SharePoint app has been added and can be found in the Apps part of your Site Contents list.

To add an app from the SharePoint Store

- First, make sure that the user account that is doing this is part of the site Owners group.
- Click **Add lists**, libraries, and other apps on the home page, next to "**Get started with your site**."

You can get started with your site control if it's not on the home page. To do this, click the Settings icon, then **View Site Contents**. Finally, on the **Site Contents** page, click **Add an App**.

- Pick the SharePoint Store.
- Look through the SharePoint Store to get the app you want.
- Pick out an app to add.
- Click on **Read More**, and then **Buy It.**
- Do what it says to do to join in and buy the app if you need to.
- If you believe the app, click **Allow Access** in the **Grant Permission to an App** dialog.

The SharePoint app has been added and can be found in the Apps part of your Site Contents list.

Branding and Theming SharePoint Sites

Creating Custom Themes for Brand Consistency

By making more color choices and text styles and adding them to the Theme Gallery, you can make your themes. After that, you can use the new color palettes and font styles when you change a design in the theming experience or when you use a theme in a program. Similarly, you can add more master pages and sample files to the Master Page Gallery if you want to have more site styles to choose from. The following list tells you where to put the files:

- **The Master Page Gallery** shows a list of all the master page files and the preview files (.preview files) that go with them. You need a master page sample file so that the master page can be seen in the **Change the look** wizard. You can also add JavaScript files and other creative tools to the Master Page Gallery.

On the Site Settings page, find Web Designer Galleries and click on Master pages. This will take you to the Master Page Gallery in SharePoint. You can also go straight to the site at *http://{SiteName}/_catalogs/masterpage/.*

- Theme Gallery shows a list of the color schemes and fonts that can be used for theming. SharePoint looks in the 15 areas to find the color schemes and fonts that are available.

On the Site Settings page, find Web Designer Galleries and click on Themes. This will take you to the Theme Gallery in SharePoint. The site can also be reached directly at *http://{SiteCollectionName}/_catalogs/theme/15/*.

- **Style library**: This is a list of the custom CSS files you want to use in the theme. You can get to the Style library right away by typing *http://SiteCollectionName/Style Library/language/Themable/* into your browser.

Don't put the custom CSS files in the Themable folder in the Master Page Gallery. Instead, put them in the Themable folder in the Style library. For the theming engine to work, CSS files must be kept in the Themable folder in the Style library.

Keep in mind that you need to post the design files before the theming engine can use them if versioning is turned on for the Master Page Gallery and the Theme Gallery.

To add a composed look

- Pick up the **gear button** and pick out **Site settings**.
- Pick **composed looks** from the **Web Designer Galleries** list.
- Pick out a new look from the list of **Composed Looks**.
- Type a name for the image in the **Title** text box.
- Type a name for the image in the Name text box. The name shows up in the design gallery and the list of Composed Looks.
- Type the **Master Page URL** into the Master Page URL text box. The URL can be a base URL.
- Type the color palette's URL (the URL to the ***.spcolor** file) into the **Theme URL text** box. The URL can be a base URL.
- Type the background image's URL into the **Image URL** text box. Here's an option. The URL can be a base URL.
- Type the font scheme's URL (the URL to the *.spfont file) into the **Font Scheme URL** text box. Here's an option. The URL can be a base URL.
- Type the number of the display order in the box that says "**Display Order**." This sets where in the design gallery the image will show up.
- Pick **Save**.

Implementing Custom CSS for Advanced Branding

A lot of what makes SharePoint look good is the cascading style sheet (CSS). It helps to know how SharePoint uses CSS so that you can change the look of your site in SharePoint and SharePoint Online. **Important**: You can only use this option for extension with the standard SharePoint experience. With current experiences in SharePoint Online, like conversation sites, you can't use this option. Also, keep in mind that you shouldn't count on the HTML page layout or the CSS style names that come with the site; these could change at any time.

CSS branding overview

Indeed, when creating a SharePoint site collection, it generates a Master Page Gallery, typically located at _catalogs/masterpage, serving as a repository for various branding assets crucial for the site's appearance and functionality. These assets may include .master, .css, image, HTML, and JavaScript files.

By default, different types of sites within SharePoint utilize specific master pages:

1. **Team Sites, Publishing Sites, and Team Sites with Publishing:** These sites default to using the seattle.master page.
2. **OneDrive for Business Sites:** OneDrive for Business sites employ the mysite15.master page.

The corev15.css file plays a pivotal role in the styling of SharePoint sites. It is composed of various .css files that are integral to the default styling in SharePoint. Each .master file within the Master Page Gallery references the corev15.css file. When it comes to styling, all default master pages leverage the corev15.css file. The application of styles is facilitated through the CSS cascade and CSS file sharing mechanisms, allowing SharePoint to determine which styles are applied to different controls and features throughout a page. Additionally, the oslo.css file, associated with the oslo.master master page, is constructed from several CSS files amalgamated to achieve the desired styling for sites using this master page. Understanding the role of these master pages and associated CSS files is essential for effectively customizing and branding SharePoint sites to meet specific design and functional requirements.

To create a custom style sheet for SharePoint

- Copy **corev15.css** and name it **contosov15.css**.
- As shown in the next example, open the correct masterpage (in this case, contoso.masterpage) and change the CssRegistration line to point to contosov15.css instead of corev15.css.

```XML
<SharePoint:CssRegistration Name="Themable/contoso.css" runat="server" />
```

- These should be added below the line that says "CSSRegistration."

```XML
<SharePoint:CssRegistration name="/_catalogs/masterpage/contoso/contoso.css"
runat="server">
```

Composed looks in custom branding

When CSS is called from a master page, you can use combined looks in custom branding. One of the following places in the SharePoint file system is where the CSS file is kept:

- 15\TEMPLATE\LAYOUTS\{LCID}\STYLES\Themable
- /Style Library/Themable/
- /Style Library/{culture}/Themable/

Custom branding files can be stored in /Style Library/Themable and /Style Library/{culture}/Themable. However, 15\TEMPLATE\LAYOUTS\{LCID}\STYLES\Themable can't be changed, so you can't put custom files there.

CHAPTER 7

WORKFLOW AUTOMATION IN SHAREPOINT

Introduction to SharePoint Workflows

Workflow is sometimes thought of as a set of tasks that work together to make something happen. Workflow is more specifically used in SharePoint Products and Technologies to mean the automatic moving of papers or things through a set of business-related actions or tasks. Organizations can use workflows to handle common business processes regularly. This is done by adding business logic to papers or items in a SharePoint library or list. Business logic is simply a list of rules that tells a document or thing what to do and how to do it. By handling and keeping track of the people who do the work that goes into common business processes like project approval or document review, workflows can cut down on the time and money needed to handle these processes. In a SharePoint site, for instance, you can add a process to a document library that sends a document to a group of people to accept. When a document author starts this workflow on a document in that library, the workflow makes document approval tasks and gives them to the people who are part of the workflow. The participants are then sent emails with directions on how to complete the tasks and a link to the document that needs to be approved. The document author is the workflow owner in this case. He or she or the other people in the workflow can check the Workflow Status page at any time to see who has finished their jobs. When everyone in the workflow finishes their jobs, the workflow stops, and the owner of the workflow is instantly told that it's over. The steps taken in the Approval routine in the last example are similar to those in the next case.

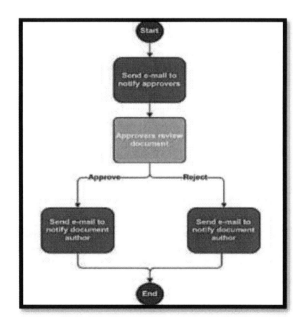

You can use workflows to support the way you already work, and they also let you work together on papers, lists, and libraries in new ways. Users of the site can start processes and take part in them by using forms that can be changed and that can be accessed from a document or item in a SharePoint library or list.

Built-in workflows

Some built-in processes in SharePoint sites can be used to handle common business situations.

- **Approval**: This process sends a file or thing to a group of people to be reviewed. The Approval process is linked to the Document content type by default, so it can be found in document files without any extra work.
- **Collect Feedback**: This process sends a file or thing to a group of people to get feedback. Reviewers can give their thoughts, which are then put together and sent to the person who started the process. Because the Collect Feedback process is linked to the Document content type by default, it can be found in document files.
- **Collect Signatures**: This process sends a Microsoft Office file to a group of people so that their digital signatures can be added. To finish their signing jobs, participants must use the right Office software to add their digital signature to the paper. Because the Collect Signatures process is linked to the Document content type by default, it can be found in document files. The Collect Signatures process, on the other hand, only shows up for a document in the document library if it has at least one Microsoft Office Signature Line.
- **Publishing permission**: This is like the Approval workflow in that it automatically sends material to experts and stakeholders for review and permission. The publishing review process is special because it was made for publishing sites that strictly control when new and changed web pages are published.
- **Three-state**: This procedure can be used to handle business processes that need to keep track of a lot of problems or things, like project chores, sales leads, or customer service issues.

There are several ways that you can change each of the above processes to fit your business. In this case, you can change the project lists and history lists that hold information about the process after adding it to a list, library, or content type so that it can be used on papers or items. When a user on the site starts a process on a document or item, they may have the option to make it even more unique by choosing the list of partners, the due date, and the job directions.

Steps involved in using workflows

Using workflows in SharePoint involves several steps, each carried out by individuals with different roles. Here's an overview of the key steps involved in implementing workflows:

1. **Adding a Workflow to a List, Library, or Content Type:**

- Before a workflow can be utilized, it needs to be associated with a list, library, or content type. This step makes the workflow available for documents or items in a specific location.
- Adding a workflow to a list, library, or content type typically requires the Manage Lists permission, and it is often performed by site managers or individuals responsible for specific lists or libraries.
- There are different places on a site where a workflow can be added, impacting its availability:
    - If added to a list or library, the workflow can only be used for items within that list or library.
    - Adding a workflow to a list content type means it will only work for items of that content type within the specific list or library.
    - A site workflow can be created to be available across multiple lists or libraries within a site.

2. **Configuring Workflow Options:**
    - When adding a workflow to a list, library, or content type, various configuration options are available:
        - **Instance Name:** Naming the specific instance of the workflow.
        - **Task List:** Specifying the list where work-related tasks will be stored.
        - **History List:** Designating the list that tracks all events that occur during the workflow.
        - **Start Options:** Defining how the workflow should commence.
        - Other workflow-specific options that vary depending on the nature of the workflow.

3. **Making Workflows Available:**
    - Adding a workflow to a list, library, or content type doesn't initiate the workflow itself; instead, it makes the workflow available for use on documents or items in that particular location.

4. **Roles in Workflow Execution:**
    - Different individuals may be involved in different stages of the workflow:
        - Site owners can make workflows available in document libraries.
        - Content authors can initiate or make changes to ongoing workflows.
        - Document reviewers or approvers can complete workflow tasks.

By following these steps, organizations can effectively leverage workflows in SharePoint to streamline and automate business processes, ensuring efficient collaboration and task management.

Introduction to Power Automate

Power Automate is a powerful and flexible Microsoft tool that is an important part of managing processes, even those that are connected to SharePoint. Users of this tool can simplify processes and make jobs easier without having to know a lot about code.

Power Automate lets you make automatic processes, or **"flows,"** that are tailored to your needs. These flows can start when certain things happen, like when a document changes or when something new is added. Power handle works perfectly with SharePoint and lets users handle tasks related to managing documents, updating lists, and other SharePoint features. Data handling and collaboration are made easier by this connection. SharePoint has many events that can start flows, such as when an item is created, changed, or deleted. This makes sure that the system works perfectly with the changes or conditions that are wanted in the SharePoint setting. Power Automate comes with a huge library of actions and conditions that users can use in their processes. Some of these acts are very simple, like making a thing, and some are more complicated, like sending alerts or changing records. With Power Automate, users can set up review processes without any problems. This is especially helpful when paper reviews or decision-making processes are important to running a business.

How to Create a Workflow for a List or Library

1. Pick out the library for which you want to make the flow.
2. Find **Power Automate** under the **Automate** option in the command bar.
3. Press **"Create a flow."**
4. From the list on the right, choose a flow template. You can use one of the pre-made flows or build your own from scratch.
5. You can link Power Automate to a SharePoint list or library.
6. You should be taken to the creator for Power Automate. You should be able to change how your process works once you get here.
   - Your process starts with the first step in the flow, which is called the trigger. After the first move, you can add more. All of these depend on what was done before.
   - One kind of flow happens on its own when something is added or changed. You can only start a second type of flow after you choose an item.
     - In SharePoint, click the Automate button in the command bar to start this flow. The type of trigger you chose before will determine whether the flow starts itself or you have to start it from the command bar.
     - Fill in any blanks with your information or change the template's default settings. Click **Edit** next to **Send Email** to change the usual settings. You can change how the email looks and show extra fields from the SharePoint item using the options for the **Send Email** action.
7. Set up the flow, and then click **"Create Flow."**
8. Click **"Done"** when you're done making the flow.

If you want to make processes for any list or library in your SharePoint site, follow these general steps. When you are building a flow for a list or library in SharePoint, make sure to follow these steps.

How to Create a Simple Approval Workflow in SharePoint

The review process can be done automatically with this great, simple method. This way, people in your company don't have to play email tag to get a paper or file approved.

1. Start up the **SharePoint Designer**.
2. Go to your SharePoint site, click **File**, and then click **Open**.
3. Go to your list of tasks and check the box next to Need content approval for filed things.
4. Click **New Item** on the **File** tab. Pick out the process list. Give your new review process a name and a list of things to do.
5. Press the **Workflow settings** button and then check the boxes in the **Start Options** area that need to be checked.
6. Go back to changing your process for approval. In Step 1, click on Action and then pick the **Set Workflow variable.**
7. Go to process variables and click on make new variables. Type in the variable's name and pick its type from the list.
8. Go to **Value** and set up the process look-up.
9. Make the condition part of this move.
10. Say what the first connection is worth. Pick the **Data Source and Field** from the source from the drop-down options, and then click **OK**.
11. Type in a number for this second link, and then click **OK**.
12. Add the action that needs to be done to this link.
13. To this condition, add the action *Set Content Approval Status*. Click on the status link to set the approval state and add some notes.
14. Click on **Check for Errors**. If there are no mistakes, click "**Save**" and then "**Publish**" to start the review process.

CHAPTER 8
ADVANCED DOCUMENT MANAGEMENT
Document Sets and Content Organizer

For many types of projects, people make a bunch of papers that go together. Some projects end with this set of papers, which is also known as the "deliverable." A common "pitch book" is one thing that a professional services company might make when they answer a possible client's request for a proposal.

There may always be these parts in the pitch book, with each one being changed to fit the needs of the current project:

- An introduction to the services company
- A Strengths, Weaknesses, Opportunities, and Threats (SWOT) analysis
- A business plan
- A comparable company analysis

In other situations, this group of papers may only contain different kinds of data that help with a bigger project and lead to the creation or release of something else. For instance, a company that makes things might make a regular set of papers for each product that it makes that deal with creation, testing, and production. These papers can be made all at once or in stages. Individuals or groups may create or review the papers. The style of all the files might be the same, like Word files. They could also be different file types, like Word papers, OneNote notes, PowerPoint slideshows, Visio models, Excel worksheets, and so on. Document Sets can make it easier for businesses to handle these scenarios. Multiple documents that are linked are put together in a single view by the Document Set so that they can be worked on and handled as a single unit. It's a new content type that you make when you make a new **Document Set**. The content type is then available across the whole site collection. For each multi-document work product, you can set up a new Document Set content type. Users can make new instances of the Document Set the same way they make new instances of a single document after adding a Document Set content type to a library.

What can you do with a Document Set?

There are some aspects of the Document Set content type that make it easier to make and handle work products with multiple documents. **You can do any of the following when you set up a Document Set content type:**

- **Customize a Welcome Page**: Change the Document Set's Welcome Page so that it has all the details a person needs about the set. The Welcome Page is a Web Part Page that can be set up to show project details or resources that will help team members working on a Document Set. For example, it could show the project schedule or links to resources. It also shows a list of the new files that were added to the set.

- **Specify default content**: You can choose what **basic content** you want to be made and added to every new copy of the Document Set. You can make some papers appear instantly, and you can decide which designs people use. You can be sure that the content types of the basic papers are right. One example is that when you set up a Document Set content type, you can share unique files that your company uses for certain types of communication.
- **Specify allowed content types**: Choose the types of content that can be used in the document set, like text files, pictures, sound files, or videos.
- **Specify shared metadata**: Choose the information fields and common metadata that you want for all the documents in a set. When the Document Set is made, the metadata is added to the default documents immediately. You can also see the shared information on the Welcome page.
- **Specify shared metadata**: Set up the processes you want to use for the Document Set. With Document Sets, you can use the standard Review or Approval processes. The whole Document Set will go through the workflow steps as if it were a single file. In addition, your company can create its processes for Document Sets.

Send Document Sets to the Content Organizer so that they can be sent to a specific library, site, or area.

Enable Document Sets for a site collection

Before you can make or set up new Document Set content types, you will need to make sure that the Document Sets feature is turned on for your site collection. **To use the Document Sets tool, you need to be a Site Collection Administrator.**

- Find the major site in the group of sites that you want to use Document Sets for.
- Select Site Settings from the list of actions on the site.
- Go to **Site Collection Administration** and click on **Site Group Features**.
- Look for Document Sets in the list, and then press **Activate**.

Create a new Document Set content type

To let site users use Document Sets to make new multi-document work products, you must first make and set up a Document Set content type for each work product you want to handle. Then, you must add the Document Set content type to the document library where it will be used. You need to add the Document Set content type to the library where users can make their own Document Sets after you've made it and set it up.

To make or change Document Set content types, you need to be a Site Collection Administrator or a Site Owner.

1. Go to the **Site Actions** menu and click on **Site Settings**.
2. Select Site content types from the list of galleries.
3. Turn to the Site Content Types page and click the Create button.
4. Under "**Name and Description**," put the name you want to give your new Document Set in the "Name" box. These are the names that people will see when they make a new Document Set.
5. Type a short statement of the Document Set in the box that says "**Description.**"
6. Click **Document Set Content Types** under **Choose parent content type from**. Document Sets may not be turned on for this site group if **Document Set Content Types** is not an option.
7. In the Group area, choose whether to add your new Document Set content type to a brand-new group or an old one.
8. Click the **OK** button.

After creating a new Document Set content type, you will be taken to the Site Content Type information page for that type, where you can change some more settings.

Configure or customize a Document Set content type

1. Go to the **Site Actions** menu and click on **Site Setting**s.
2. Select **Site content types** from the galleries section.
3. Click on the name of the Document Set content type you want to change on the Site Content Types page.
4. Go to **Settings** and click on **Document Set settings**.
5. Choose the content type you want to let into this **Document Set** from the list of **Available Site Content Types** in the **Allowed Content** Types section. Then, hit the "**Add**" button to add it to the list of **Content Types allowed in the Document Set** box. Do this step again for every type of information you want to add to the Document Set.

Please note that the Allowed Content Types setting only works for documents that were added to the document set through the "**New**" button.

6. In the **Default Content** area, choose the type of content for which you want to add default content. Then, click **Browse** to find the file you want to add. When writers make new copies of a Document Set, default content is made for them immediately.

Let's say you are making a Document Set to keep track of the process of designing a product. There may be a Product Design Document (a Microsoft Word file), a Design Drawing (a Microsoft Visio file), and Performance Specs (a Microsoft Excel worksheet) in this Document Set. There may be a standard Microsoft Word example for the Product Design Document in your company that already has some of the standard information that writers need to fill in. You can set this design

103

as the usual text. Authors get a copy of the Product Design Document when they make a new version of the product design Document Set. They can change it to add more information. If you don't include default content for the content types in the Document Set, authors will not be able to automatically create files when they create a new instance of a Document Set. Instead, authors will have to make them from scratch within the Document Set or upload documents to it.

7. If this Document Set has more than one type of content, and you want to add default content for each one, click **"Add new default content,"** choose the type of content you want to add default content for, and then click **"Browse"** to find the file you want to share. Do this step again and again until you've set all of the default content you want for each type of content in this Document Set.
8. Select the check box next to **Add the name of the Document Set** to **each file name** if you want the name of the Document Set to appear in the names of the files that are part of a Document Set. Adding this information could help users find files in some library views, especially if the library has more than one type of Document Set.
9. Under **"Shared Columns,"** pick the columns that you want all of the content types in the Document Set to share.

The documents in the Document Set can only read shared fields, and only the Document Set itself can change them. If the values of the shared columns for the Document Set are changed, these changes will also be made to the values of the shared columns for the documents in the set.

10. Choose which columns you want to show on the Document Set's Welcome Page in the **Welcome Page Columns** area.
11. Elsewhere in the Document Set, click Customize the Welcome Page in the Welcome Page part to change how the Welcome Page looks for each version of the Document Set.
12. If you want these changes to be made to all Document Sets that come from this Document Set, check the box next to **Update the Welcome Page of Document Sets inheriting from this content type**.
13. In the **Update List and Site Content Types** area, choose which content types that come from this Document Set you want to have the changes you made applied to them.
14. Press **"OK."**

You need to add the Document Set content type to the library where users can make their own Document Sets after you've made it and set it up.

Content Organizer

The Content Organizer is a part of SharePoint that can handle some important library chores instantly. This can help make sure that a document library is handled regularly and saves time.

What can the Content Organizer do?

The Content Organizer in SharePoint serves as an automated system that can perform several tasks independently, enhancing document management and organization. **Here are the key functionalities of the Content Organizer:**

1. **Route Documents to Different Libraries or Folders:**
   - Acting as a guardian for documents, the Content Organizer utilizes predefined rules to automatically determine the appropriate destination for each new document.
   - Documents can be routed to different libraries or folders, even across site collections, based on metadata and other specified criteria.

2. **Upload Documents to a Drop-Off Library:**
   - The Content Organizer can be configured to direct all incoming documents to a designated Drop-Off Library.
   - This Drop-Off Library serves as a central location where additional information can be added, and the submission process can be completed before documents are further distributed.

3. **Manage Folder Size:**
   - Content Organizer can monitor folders for capacity and prevent them from exceeding a specified limit, often set by default to 2500 items.
   - When a folder reaches its limit, the Content Organizer automatically creates a new folder and transfers the document to maintain an organized structure.
   - Administrators can configure the system to determine the maximum number of items allowed in a single folder.

4. **Manage Duplicate Submissions:**
   - To handle situations where a user uploads a document that already exists in the library, the Content Organizer provides options to manage duplicates.
   - Administrators can instruct the system to use a different version of the file or add unique characters to the file name, ensuring both the original and the copy are retained securely.

5. **Maintain Audit Logs:**
   - Content Organizer can generate and maintain audit logs for each document it processes.
   - These logs contain information about the document's journey, providing an audit trail that can be valuable for tracking and compliance purposes.

Activate the Content Organizer feature on a site

To activate and configure the Content Organizer tool on a SharePoint site, follow these steps:

1. **Ensure Prerequisites:**

- Ensure that the posting tools are turned on, and you have at least Site Owner permissions to modify settings.

2. **Navigate to Site Settings:**
   - Go to the site for which you want to change settings.

3. **Access Site Settings:**
   - Click on "Settings" (gear icon), and from the drop-down menu, select "Site settings."
   - Alternatively, go to "Settings," click on "Site contents," and then click on "Site settings."

4. **Access Manage Site Features:**
   - On the Site Settings page, locate the "Site Actions" group.
   - Click on "Manage site features" within this group.

5. **Activate Content Organizer:**
   - Look for the Content Organizer function in the list of features.
   - Click the "Activate" button next to the name of the Content Organizer function.

6. **Verify Activation:**
   - Once activated, the word "Active" will appear in the Status section, indicating that the Content Organizer feature is now turned on for the site.

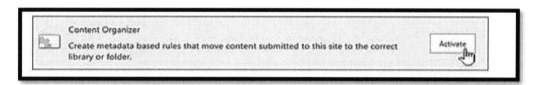

Configure the Content Organizer to route documents

To set up the Content Organizer in SharePoint, follow these steps:

1. **Ensure Permissions:**
   - Make sure you have at least Site Owner permissions to set up the Content Organizer.

2. **Navigate to Site Settings:**
   - Go to the site where you want to configure the Content Organizer.

3. **Access Site Settings:**
   - Click on "Settings" (gear icon), and from the drop-down menu, select "Site settings."
   - Alternatively, go to "Settings," click on "Site contents," and then click on "Site settings."

4. **Access Content Organizer Settings:**
   - Click on "Content Organizer Settings" in the Site Administration group.
   - Note: The Content Organizer settings link will only be visible if the tool is turned on for the site.

5. **Configure Content Organizer Settings:**
   - Check the box to make the Content Organizer mandatory in the "Redirect Users to the Drop off Library" section. This ensures that when users attempt to share a file, they are directed immediately to the Drop-Off Library.
   - Check the "Allow Rules to Send Documents to a Different Site" box in the "Sending to Another Site" section.
   - In the "Folder Partitioning" section:
     - Check the box next to "Create subfolders after a target location has too many items." This creates subfolders when a location surpasses a specified item limit.
     - Specify the number of items in a single folder before a new one is created in the "Number of things in a single folder" box.
     - Choose the desired format for the new folder names in the "Format of folder name" box.
6. **Manage Duplicate Submissions:**
   - Under "Duplicate Submissions," choose whether duplicates should use versioning or have file names that always start with a different set of characters.
7. **Preserving Context:**
   - If you want to save audit logs or information as an audit record on the filed item or document, check the box in the "Preserving Context" area.
8. **Rule Managers:**
   - In the "Rule Managers" area, enter the names of individuals in your company who are responsible for managing rules. Rule makers must have "Manage Web Site" permissions to access the Content Organizer rules setting page.
   - If configured correctly, emails can be sent immediately to rule makers when content is sent to the Content Organizer or when content doesn't meet a rule. Note: Email options require proper setup by your SharePoint or network administrator.
9. **Submission Points:**
   - Fill out the "Submission Points" area with information about other websites or email clients that can send content to this one.

Information Rights Management (IRM)

Your users can't do certain things with downloaded files from lists or libraries when you use information rights management (IRM). Some certain people and apps are not allowed to decrypt downloaded files because of IRM. The people who are allowed to read files can also have their rights limited by IRM. This means that they can't do things like make copies of the files or copy text from them. IRM can be used on libraries or lists to stop private information from getting out to too many people. For instance, if you're making a document library to share information about new goods with certain marketing representatives, you can use IRM to stop these reps from sharing this information with other workers of the company. On a site, you use IRM on a list or library as whole, not just on individual files. It's now easier to make sure that all of your papers and files are always protected at the same level. Therefore, IRM can assist your company in upholding the rules that control the sharing and use of private or secret data. IRM safety is put on files in SharePoint Online at the list and library levels. As a business, you need to set up Rights Management before you can use IRM safety. The Azure Rights Management tool from Azure Information Protection is what IRM uses to secure data and set limits on how it can be used. Not all Microsoft 365 plans come with Azure Rights Management. Tip: If you're not a user of E5, you can try out Microsoft Purview products for free for 90 days to see how other Purview features can help your business with data security and compliance.

How IRM can help protect content

IRM helps to protect restricted content in the following ways:

- Helps stop authorized viewers from copying, editing, printing, faxing, or copying and pasting the content for illegal use.
- Helps stop authorized viewers from copying the content by using Microsoft Windows' **Print Screen** feature.
- Helps stop unauthorized viewers from viewing the content if it is sent by email after being downloaded from the server.
- Limits access to content for a certain amount of time, after which users must log out.
- Helps your company follow the rules for how material can be used and shared within the company

How IRM cannot help protect content

IRM cannot protect restricted content from the following:

- Malicious programs like Trojan horses, keystroke hackers, and some kinds of spyware can delete, steal, record, or send data.
- Computer viruses can also damage or delete data.
- Copying the content on a screen by hand or typing it again;
- Taking pictures of the content on a screen, either digitally or on film;
- Copying with third-party screen-capture programs;
- Copying content metadata (column values) with third-party screen-capture programs or by copying and pasting;

Turn on IRM service using the SharePoint admin center

You must first turn on the **Rights Management** service for your company before you can IRM-protect SharePoint lists and libraries. To turn on the Rights Management service, you need to use a work or school account that has global management rights. You will not be able to use IRM tools with SharePoint Online if you don't do this.

Once the Rights Management service is up and running, go to the SharePoint admin center and log in to turn on IRM.

1. Log in as a SharePoint manager or a global admin.
2. To open the Microsoft 365 admin center, click the app launcher button in the top left corner and select **Admin**. If you don't see the **Admin tile**, it means that your work or school account doesn't have the right permissions to be an administrator in your company.
3. Click **Admin centers > SharePoint admin center** on the left side of the screen.
4. Go to the settings menu on the left side of the screen and select the old settings page.
5. Under **Information Rights Management (IRM),** pick Use the IRM service that was set up in your setup. Next, pick Refresh IRM Settings. After you update the IRM settings, people in your company can use IRM in their SharePoint files and lists. But in Library Settings and List Settings, the options to do that might not show up for up to an hour.

IRM-enable SharePoint document libraries and lists

Site owners can IRM-protect their SharePoint files and lists after updating their IRM settings. If a site owner turns on IRM for a list or library, they can protect any file types that are allowed by that list or library. All the files in a library are subject to rights management when IRM is turned on for that library. When you turn on IRM for a list, it only manages the files that are connected to list items. It doesn't manage the list of items themselves.

The files are secured so that only allowed users can view them when people download files from an IRM-enabled list or library. Every file that is handled by rights also has an issue license that limits who can view the file. Some common limits are making a file read-only, stopping people from copying text, stopping them from saving a local copy, and stopping them from printing the file. The issued license in the rights-managed file is used by client programs that can read IRM-supported file types to implement these limits. In this way, a rights-managed file stays safe even after it has been downloaded.

If your library has IRM, you can't use Office in a browser to make or change documents in that library. IRM-encrypted files can only be downloaded and changed by one person at a time. Check-in and check-out are used to handle co-authoring, which is when more than one person writes the same thing. It makes a protected PDF file when you download a PDF file from an IRM-protected library in Microsoft 365. The name of the file won't change, but the file is safe. You'll need the Azure Information Protection browser, the full Azure Information Protection client, or another program that can open protected PDF files to view this file.

The following file types can be encrypted in SharePoint Online:

*   PDF
*   The Microsoft Office 97–2003 file types for the following programs: There's PowerPoint, Word, and Excel.

- The Office Open XML file types for these Microsoft Office programs: There's PowerPoint, Word, and Excel.
- The XML Paper Specification (XPS) format

Keep in mind that IRM protection can't be used on protected files like digitally signed PDFs because SharePoint needs to open the file when it is uploaded.

Next steps

You can start managing rights for lists and libraries once you've turned on IRM for SharePoint Online. It is now possible for the new OneDrive sync client for Windows to sync IRM-protected SharePoint document libraries with OneDrive locations, as long as the library's IRM setting isn't set to end document access rights.

Applying IRM to Document Libraries and Lists

If you want to keep things you download from lists or libraries safe, you can use Information Rights Management (IRM). The Microsoft global cloud is the only place where this tool works. In national cloud applications, IRM does not work with SharePoint lists and libraries.

Administrator preparations before applying IRM

- Information Rights Management for sites can be done with the Azure Rights Management service (Azure RMS) from Azure Information Protection and the on-premises version, Active Directory Rights Management Services (AD RMS). There is no need for any different or extra installs.
- You need to turn on IRM for your site before you can use it on a list or library. To activate IRM, you must have management permissions.
- To add IRM to a library or list, you must have administrator permissions for that library or list.
- When your users try to download bigger IRM-protected files in SharePoint Online, they may run into timeouts. To escape timeouts, protect bigger files with IRM in Office and store them in a SharePoint library that doesn't use IRM.

Apply IRM to a list or library

1. Find the list or library that you want to set up IRM for.
2. Click the **Library tab** on the menu and then click **Library Settings**. To change the settings for a list, go to the List tab and then pick List Settings.

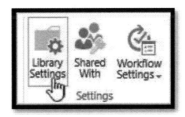

3. Choose **Information Rights Management** from the list of **Permissions and Management**. It's possible that IRM is not turned on for your site if the Information Rights Management link doesn't show up. Talk to the person who runs the server to find out if you can turn on IRM for your site. For picture galleries, the link for **Information Rights Management** doesn't show up.
4. On the page for **Information Rights Management Settings**, check the box next to **Restrict permission to documents in this library on download**. This will limit the users' access to documents they download from this list or library.
5. In the box that says "**Create a permission policy title**," give the policy a name that tells you what it does. Give this strategy a name that makes it easy to tell apart from others. To give a list or library that includes private company papers limited permissions, for instance, use Company Confidential.

6. Type a description of how people who use this list or library should handle the documents in it in the "**Add a permission policy description**" box. This description will show up for people who use the list or library. For instance, you can type **Discuss the contents of this document only with other employees** if you only want internal employees to be able to see the information in these documents.
7. Choose **Show Options** and follow any instructions that are presented to you to add more limits to the files in this list or library.
8. Once you've chosen all the options you want, click **OK**.

Document Retention

By using a retention strategy or retention label, you can keep all of the files that are saved in SharePoint sites. Along with live sites, archived sites can be used.

The following files can be deleted:

- When you have a method for keeping records: All the files in document libraries, including any SharePoint document libraries that are made automatically, like Site Assets.
- When you need to use retention labels: Every file in every document library and every file at the top level that isn't in a folder.

SharePoint will make a Preservation Hold library for the site if one doesn't already exist so that information that needs to be kept can be kept. The Preservation Hold library is a secret part of the system that isn't meant to be used directly. Instead, it saves files automatically when compliance requirements require it. It is not possible to change, remove, or move these files that are automatically kept. To get to these files, you should instead use compliance tools, like those that work with eDiscovery.

With the help of preservation rules and labels, the Preservation Hold library works like this:

People can change or remove items that need to be kept because of a retention policy or a retention label that says they are records. When they do either of those things, the original content is copied to the Preservation Hold library. Users can change or remove information in their app with this behavior, but they must keep a copy of the original for legal reasons. The **Preservation Hold library** has a timed job that runs every so often. If the item has been in the Preservation Hold library for more than 30 days, this job checks it against all the questions that were used by the content's retention settings. When they reach the end of their set holding time, content that isn't waiting for a disposition review is removed from both the Preservation Hold library and the original place, if it is still there. If this job is run every week, it will take at least 30 days for the material to be removed from the Preservation Hold library. In total, it could take up to 37 days. When you put files into the Preservation Hold library, this is how it works for material that was there when the preservation settings were set. For retention policies, any new content added to the site or made after the policy was put in place will also be kept in the Preservation

Hold library. The first-time new content is changed; however, it is not copied to the Preservation Hold library. Only when new content is destroyed is it copied. Versioning must be turned on for the source site to keep all copies of a file. Users get a message when they try to delete a site, library, list, or folder that can be kept. The person can get rid of an unnamed folder as long as they move or delete any files in it that need to be kept. Users will also get an error message if they try to delete a named item in any of the situations below. **The item stays where it was found and is not copied to the Preservation Hold library:**

- The setting for managing records that lets users get rid of named things has been turned off.

In the Microsoft Purview compliance interface, go to the Records management solution and change or check this setting. Then, go to **Records management > Records management settings > Retention labels > Deletion of items**. SharePoint and OneDrive each have their settings. Let's say you don't have access to the Records control system. You can still use **AllowFilesWithKeepLabelToBeD.**You can use Get-PnPTenant and Set-PnPTenant to select SPO and **A** *lowFilesWithKeepLabelToBeDeletedODB*.

- The hold sticker says that the item is a record and locks it.

There is a copy of the most recent version kept in the Preservation Hold library until the record is opened.

- The retention label indicates that the item is a regulatory record, which means it can't be changed or removed.

It depends on whether the preservation settings are to keep and delete, keep only, or delete only that content in a OneDrive account or SharePoint site. The content then goes in one of three different ways. As we'll see, changed content is moved to the Preservation Hold library for rules on record retention. Items are marked as records with retention labels, and the content is made available. When items are removed, copies are made in the Preservation Hold library, but not when items are changed with retention labels that don't mark them as records. **When the settings for keeping are to keep and delete:**

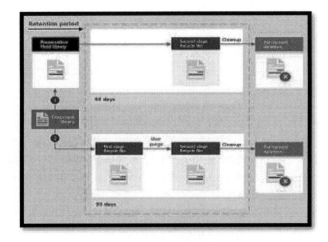

113

1. *If the content is changed or removed* during the retention time, the Preservation Hold library makes a copy of the original content as it was when the retention settings were set. That's where the timer job finds things whose holding period has ended. Things like that are sent to the second-stage Recycle Bin, and after 93 days, they are removed for good. End users can only see the first-stage Recycle Bin; they can't see the second-stage Recycle Bin. However, site collection admins can view and recover material from that bin.

Note: We no longer remove content forever from the Preservation Hold library so that data doesn't get lost by accident. Instead, we only clear content from the Recycle Bin for good. This means that all content from the Preservation Hold library now goes through the second-stage Recycle Bin.

2. At the end of the holding period, ***if the content wasn't changed or removed***, the timer job moves it to the first-stage recycle bin. People who empty this Recycle Bin (also called "purging") or remove the information in it move the document to the second-stage Recycle Bin. In both the first- and second-stage recycle bins, the trash is kept for 93 days. When the 93-day period is up, the document is deleted for good from either the first-stage or second-stage Recycle Bin. Because it isn't listed, you can't look in the Recycle Bin. Because of this, an eDiscovery search can't find any material in the Recycle Bin that should be held.

Note: The first principle of retention says that final elimination must always be put on hold if the same item needs to be kept because of another retention policy or label, or if it is on hold for legal or research reasons in eDiscovery.

CHAPTER 9

BUSINESS INTELLIGENCE WITH SHAREPOINT

Introduction to SharePoint Business Intelligence

Scorecards, dashboards, and reports are the components that makeup business intelligence. These tools are used to make choices and monitor performance. The responsibility of developing business-savvy content can be assigned to a single individual or a group of individuals, depending on the organizational structure of your company. Because it enables them to share, consume, and manage useful information, enterprises must have a BI Center site similar to SharePoint.

Learning about the Core Features

With time, Microsoft has added the following core features:

Excel Services

The good news is that you can simply implement centralized business intelligence if you have been utilizing Microsoft Excel to organize, display, and update data. If you deal with relatively modest amounts of data, you can readily include centralized business intelligence. What you can do is publish the Excel data on a SharePoint document library with the appropriate security controls. This is an alternative to attaching the Excel data to an email. Because of this, it will be simple for workers to view the data and make use of it in accordance with their requirements. SharePoint is a wonderful platform because it allows Excel documents to keep their data links intact, and the reader can view the changes as they occur in real-time. Workbooks are equipped with data models that incorporate information from a variety of sources, including SQL Server, Access, and XML as well. To make it simpler for the user to look at the information you are attempting to emphasize, you can also control the view of Excel to a Single PivotChart. Users who have the Office online App will be able to simply interact with the data from the online browser, which will help them save a significant amount of time and effort. Excel Services is only affected by one problem, and that is the fact that it is now a component of Office Online Server rather than SharePoint services. This is the sole problem with Excel Services.

PerformancePoint

The Core On-Premises data may be utilized and studied as it is shown on the dashboards thanks to PerformancePoint, which is a strategic data and analysis tool. PerformancePoint makes it possible to use and analyze the data. To suggest that it is the Cadillac of business intelligence at Microsoft would not be an offense. The core design application can be used to transmit reports and data into SharePoint, which can then be utilized to get an in-depth analysis. Users can make rational business choices that are connected to the organization's vision, goal, and long-term strategy as a result of its extensive connection with a data warehouse. This connectivity makes it feasible for users to make these judgments. Furthermore, the basic components make it possible to include web parts into SharePoint to provide online services.

Visio Services

SharePoint was updated in 2013 to include this feature, which was designed to facilitate the viewing of data. It is equipped with a variety of tools that enable the creation of comprehensive diagrams and the mapping of data inside the canvas where it is shown. The diagrams have a high resolution, which enables people to see it and interact with it even if they do not have a local view of the area. With the assistance of web component connections and JavaScript, these diagrams can be quickly expanded, which contributes to an improvement in the overall accessibility of the user experience. The incorporation of this into Business Intelligence was a fantastic concept since it enables workers to generate original ideas that are tailored precisely to the business and industry in which they work.

PowerPivot

The year 2013 saw the incorporation of this component into SharePoint, which is an efficient tool that manages the work of a vast dataset. This is because it is connected to Excel Data, which provides the highest level of control over the charts and makes it easy to pivot data with ease. It might be a client-side program or an add-on function for Excel, depending on how it was created.

Microsoft Power BI

Through the use of Power BI, it is possible to share your data with all of the personnel located inside your firm on a variety of devices. This data can be collected, and then it can be imported into Excel. This is the greatest part. As an additional option, you can make use of several visualization mechanisms like Power View, Key Performance Indicators (KPIs) in Power Pivot, and Power Map, which will make the data accessible to all users.

SQL Server Reporting Services (SSRS)

There has been a lot of discussion on SSRS among a variety of organizations. Reports that are structured have been created by programmers and IT professionals with the assistance of this. After that, these reports are published with the assistance of a controlled environment on SharePoint sites, which provides users with an excellent experience. You must be aware that SharePoint provides excellent Business Intelligence; but, it does not yet include some of the more sophisticated capabilities that are now being offered by competing companies. Even though Microsoft is making significant investments in business intelligence, the company is primarily concentrating on cloud services, the release of SQL, and the purchase of Datazen.

Business Intelligence Center

The data that your firm has is likely stored in some forms, including databases, e-mail messages, and spreadsheet files. More specifically, your organization contains a large amount of data. You can helpfully arrange that data and show that data as information that is meaningful with the assistance of the Business Intelligence Center website and its tools. The Business Intelligence Center is a pre-built website, also known as a site template that is designed to assist you in managing the operational aspects of business intelligence (BI) reporting. These features include scorecards, dashboards, data connections, status lists, status indicators, and many more. You can personalize a Business Intelligence Center site to your liking, or you can simply begin by making use of the features that are already included in the platform. To get started, the Business Intelligence Center is an excellent location to go. An Excel Services worksheet for analysis, charts, and other types of dashboards are some examples of crucial business intelligence pieces that can be seen here. Moreover, you can click on links that are easily situated and connect to publications that provide additional information to get additional knowledge about any case. The creation of data connections, the management of information for PerformancePoint Services or SharePoint BI, and the storage of final dashboards are all possible with the help of special-purpose libraries that are already prepared for access.

On the home page of Business Intelligence, there are two primary panels: the center panel contains information resources, and the Quick Launch panel, which is located on the left side of the screen, has connections to pre-built libraries.

The center panel – examples and links to helpful information

You will get a brief overview of the Business Intelligence middle's unique features by looking at the panel in the middle of the home page. Some examples of business intelligence (BI) tools are provided by the information panels. These examples include dashboards, analytic tools, and spreadsheets. Status indicators are also included. Those who have an Enterprise license for SharePoint can get information on the simple but potent tools that are included in every installation of the platform. In addition, these information panels provide connections to information about PerformancePoint Services, which provide tools for performance monitoring and analysis that are extraordinary in their strength and sophistication.

Monitor Key Performance

- You can find links to information on various methods of monitoring performance, SharePoint Status Lists, and scorecards in PerformancePoint Services inside the Monitor Key Performance panel. These links can be found in the panel.
- The creation of SharePoint Status Lists is a simple and speedy process.
- A comprehensive hierarchical structure and a link to specialized analytical reports are also features offered by PerformancePoint scorecards.

Build and Share Reports

- There are connections to information about Excel Services and the interactive visualization tools that are included in PerformancePoint Services that can be found under the Build and Share Reports panel.
- Excel is the most widely used business intelligence tool in the world, and Excel Services gives you the ability to create your issue solution in Excel. Excel spreadsheets, PivotTables, and charts can be created, and then the reports that you create can be published to SharePoint.
- Charts and graphs that are connected to defined Key Performance Indicators, Strategy Maps, linked geographic maps, and a wide variety of additional options are included among the data visualization tools that are available in PerformancePoint Services.

Create Dashboards

- You can discover links to information on how to build dashboards by using tools in SharePoint alone or by using tools in PerformancePoint Services here in the Create Dashboards panel. These links will take you to the information you need to know.
- This panel has some buttons, one of which is titled "**Start using PerformancePoint Services**," which navigates to the homepage of the PerformancePoint Services website.
- If you want to get started right away, you can either click the **Run button** on Dashboard Designer or follow the links to the Getting Started articles. These articles will assist you in

creating scorecards, decomposition trees, dashboards, as well as analytical charts and grids.

Dashboard library

A dashboard in SharePoint is essentially a straightforward Web Part page designed to showcase a compilation of indicators, statistics, or visual elements. The fundamental structure of a dashboard comprises these essential components. To facilitate the creation and management of such dashboards, SharePoint includes the Dashboards library, specifically designed to store and generate Web Part pages dedicated to dashboard content. This can encompass dashboards created using PerformancePoint as well as Web Part pages featuring Status Lists for SharePoint status indicators. Dashboards crafted through the use of PerformancePoint Services are automatically saved in the Dashboards library whenever they are created using Dashboard Designer.

If you have previously generated dashboards, PerformancePoint Services allows you to import them. Alternatively, you have the option to construct a new dashboard from a Web Part page using the Ribbon commands available on the Dashboard list page. Moreover, the Ribbon commands on the Dashboard list page can be employed to create a Web Part page that includes a Status List for displaying SharePoint status indicators. Following this creation, you can enhance the dashboard by adding additional components such as charts, filters, and other content web parts based on your specific requirements. This flexible approach allows users to tailor dashboards to their needs, incorporating diverse elements to effectively convey information and insights.

Data Connections library

You can declare data source connections just once with the help of the Data Connection library, and then you can reuse those connections in any Web Part on the website. The **Universal Data Connection (UDC)** files, **Office Data Connection** (.odc) Files, and PerformancePoint Data Sources are all supported by the Data Connection library.

Documents library

Spreadsheets, SharePoint lists, text documents, and other types of documents may all be found in the Documents library, which acts as a central library. By creating folders inside this library, you can make it simpler to locate the information you need. You could, for instance, wish to create a folder labeled **"Excel Reports - financial" or "Status Lists for tracking,"** according to your preferences.

PerformancePoint Content list

With the help of Dashboard Designer, an analyst may construct a scorecard and report items for PerformancePoint Services, which can then be stored in the PerformancePoint Content list. As an instance, this particular graphic depicts a PerformancePoint Content library that includes a scorecard, a report, and Key Performance Indicators (KPIs).

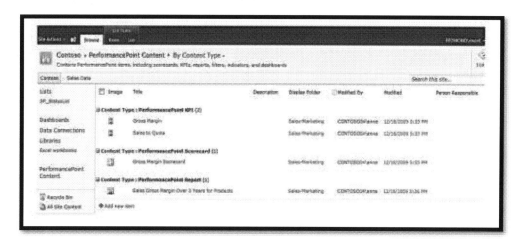

Create a new Business Intelligence Site

The Business Intelligence Center site template in SharePoint provides a dedicated and organized platform for creating and managing business intelligence solutions. SharePoint Site Owners can access this template through the New Site dialog box, enabling them to easily set up a Business Intelligence Center tailored to their organizational needs.

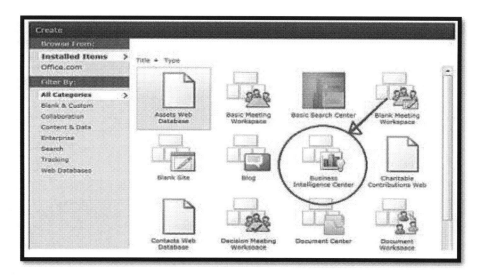

One powerful feature within the Business Intelligence Center is the ability to customize data views. This is achieved by connecting various Filter Web Parts to existing Web Parts on a dashboard page. By doing so, users can personalize the data displayed, making it more relevant and accessible to specific individuals or groups. For example, consider a scenario where different sales managers oversee distinct territories. By connecting Filter Web Parts to relevant Web Parts on the dashboard, each sales manager can have a personalized view of sales numbers specific to their region. This level of customization enhances the usability of the Business Intelligence Center, allowing stakeholders to focus on the data that matters most to them.

CHAPTER 10
SEARCH AND CONTENT DISCOVERY
Overview of Search in SharePoint

If you are in charge of search inside your business, you should educate yourself on how you can personalize the search experience to fit your organization's needs and make search even more beneficial for your users. There is a traditional search experience as well as a contemporary search experience available in SharePoint in Microsoft 365. The modern search experience provides access to Microsoft Search in SharePoint. The distinction that is most readily apparent is that the Microsoft Search box is shown in the header bar, which is located at the very top of SharePoint. The fact that Microsoft Search is a personal search is still another distinction. There is a significant difference in the results that one person gets and the results that other users receive, even when they search for identical phrases.

Before they begin entering the search box, users are presented with results that are based on their prior activity and material that is currently trending in Microsoft 365. These results are updated as the user continues to write. Because you are the administrator, the search results are simple to navigate and need no effort on your part. When it comes to finding search results, both search experiences make use of the same search index. Beyond what is possible with Microsoft Search in SharePoint, the conventional search experience can be customized and tailored to your preferences. Both experiences can be affected by some traditional search settings; it is important to understand how to prevent affecting Microsoft Search.

How search works

You will be able to have a better understanding of where and how you can adjust the search in SharePoint by reading this high-level overview of how search works.

Site columns are used to contain specific details about each document in lists and libraries.

1. The search index is updated with the site columns and values when the search crawler has completed its work on the lists and libraries.
2. Site columns are assigned to manage properties in the search index.
3. The query that is entered by a user into a search box is sent to the search index when the user inquires.
4. The search engine locates results that are a match and then directs them to a page that displays the search results.

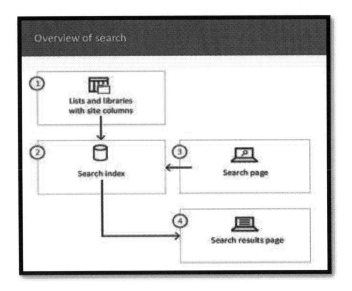

Create a custom search results page in SharePoint Online

The creation of a custom search results page for a site is one method that may be used to personalize the search experience among SharePoint users. When you use a custom page, rather than the default page that is shown in the results of Microsoft Search, you can utilize a page that you have built. Your users will have more control over the appearance of the search results experience when you utilize a page that is customized to their needs. Through the use of a custom results page, it is possible to generate a new page that can be utilized to manage the style and appearance of search results to cater to the requirements of your firm. All of the built-in web parts, as well as any open-source search web parts that have been published by the SharePoint Patterns and Practices community, as well as any custom web parts that you have written using SharePoint Framework, are options that you can employ.

Configure a results page

To configure a custom results page in SharePoint, the following procedures should be followed:

- Navigate to the website where you would want to implement a personalized results page, then navigate to the Site Settings menu, then choose Site Collection Settings, and finally select Search Settings.
- Within the Search Settings, remove the checkmark from the box that says **Use the same results page settings as my parent**, choose **Send queries to a custom results page**, and then enter a value for the column that says **Results page URL:** You should then save your modifications.

123

For example, **"https://contoso.sharepoint.com/sites/search/SitePages/results.aspx"** is an example of a URL that you should enter here. This URL should be for the page that you developed to use as your custom results page. As an alternative, you can adjust the value by using the **adjust-PnPSearchSettings SharePoint PnP PowerShell** command rather than via the Site Settings page. After it has been configured, the page that displays the results of your custom search will be shown whenever you conduct a search using the Microsoft Search box. This box is located in the navigation bar at the top of the page and is used whenever you enter search from site pages or the homepage of the website. When you are searching inside a list, library, or on the page that contains the contents of the website, you do not utilize it. You can utilize the link to broaden your search from the results of your search in lists and libraries to the page that displays your customized results.

Change the layout of your custom results page

HeaderlessSearchResults is a page layout that can be used to make the search results page look more similar to the experience that we get when we are using our out-of-box search results. This new layout can only be activated for the pages that are designated to serve as the page for the custom search results. You can use the **Set-PnPPage PnP** PowerShell command with the -**LayoutType HeaderlessSearchResults** parameter to accomplish the task of establishing the page layout.

Advanced Search Features and Syntax

The advanced search page that SharePoint provides is not the most apparent tool that the platform offers. There is no need to spell out search operators when you use advanced search since it allows you to add logic to your search. You will find that this is of tremendous assistance in limiting your results to be as suitable as possible.

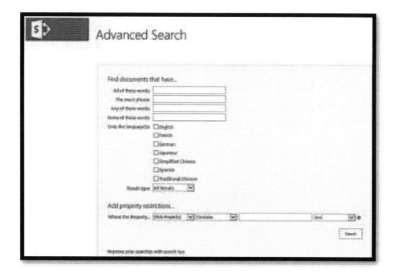

124

To a large extent, how your administrators configure your search system will determine how you can access your advanced search page. Searching for "Advanced Search" in a search box that is configured to search "Everything" should be the most effective method to get there and it should be the first result that comes up. (I am aware, really Meta). Scroll down to the bottom of any search results page and click on Advanced Search. This is yet another method for locating the page that contains the advanced search options. **You may likely access your advanced search by clicking on the following link:**

- **https://[domain].sharepoint.com/search/Pages/advanced.aspx.** Use SharePoint Online to do your search.

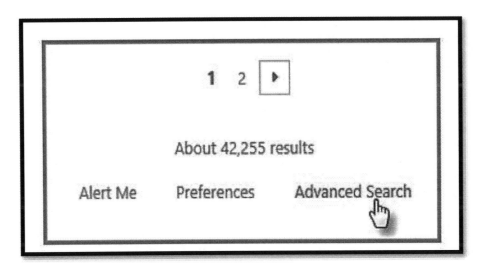

Mark that page as a bookmark or favorite, and if you want to reach it more quickly, you should probably ask your IT administrators to add a link to the homepage of the company. Continuing with the example that was shown before, here is how to use advanced search to get the same search (really, it is somewhat better). **When this occurs, the search will return results that are following the conditions listed below:**

1. Include the term "**human resources**" in its whole AND
2. Include either the word "***benefits" or "insurance***" in its entirety AND
3. Your results will not include any files that include the year 2015 AND
4. The results will only display documents (PDFs or Word docs) AND
5. The last person to modify the file has "Matt" in their name somewhere (which will return someone with the last name of "Matthew" or "Matthews") AND
6. This search will limit results to files that were last edited between 1 January 2016 and 28 February 2016 (because let's assume you know the file was last uploaded or edited in January or February 2016).

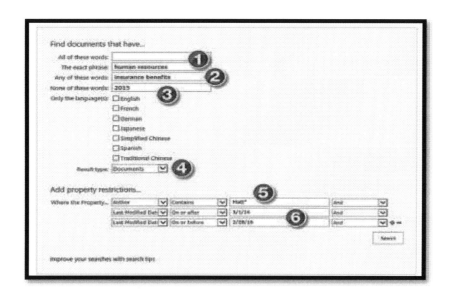

And yes, I do think that it is bothersome that the language option takes up so much space as it does when you are working in a SharePoint system with individuals who only work in one language. The fact that you have to deal with it is a given.

Results Refiners

Refiners are the most effective method for improving your results (you can find the option to use them on the page that displays your findings). They provide you the ability to filter your results by omitting date periods, file kinds, and authors that are not relevant to your search. You may either choose the author or the file type for which you want to see results, or you can adjust the scale on the changed date range. In this way, unwanted results are eliminated, and more pertinent information is brought to the surface.

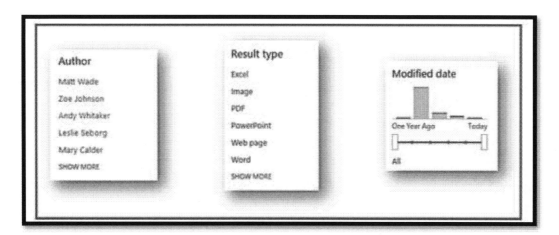

Logarithmic is the nature of the date refiner. To put it another way, it is not linear at all. Contrary to what you would believe, the points on the scale are not split in the same manner. **A general concept of how it operates may be found below.**

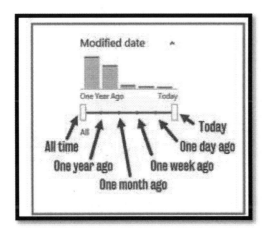

Understanding Query Syntax for Effective Search

When it comes to the construction of search queries, SharePoint search is compatible with both the Keyword Query Language (KQL) and the FAST Query Language (FQL) search syntax.

Keyword Query Language (KQL)

KQL is the query language that is used by default for constructing search queries. Specification of the search terms or property constraints that are sent to the SharePoint search service may be accomplished via the use of KQL.

FAST Query Language (FQL)

The FAST Query Language is a structured query language that allows for the addition of additional query operators. In situations where you need to write complicated queries that you want to send to the SharePoint search engine programmatically, you can make use of the FQL language. End users are not supposed to be exposed to FQL, which is why it is configured to be disabled by default. Use the EnableFQL attribute to enable FQL. Copy the default result source and then make the following modifications to the Query Transformation string {?{searchTerms} - ContentClass=urn:content-class:SPSPeople} at the Search Service Application (SSA), Site Collection, or Site levels:

- Remove the KQL filter, *-ContentClass:urn:content-class:SPSPeople*, from the Query Transformation. The resulting Query Transformation string will be: *{?{searchTerms}}*
- Replace the Query Transformation string with an FQL equivalent, such as *{?andnot({searchTerms},filter(contentclass:"urn:content-class:SPSPeople*"))}*.

CHAPTER 11
RECORDS MANAGEMENT AND ARCHIVING
Records Management Overview

A record is an item in an organization, whether it's a paper copy or a computer file that shows what the organization did or bought and needs to be kept for a certain amount of time. As a company grows, it decides what kinds of information should be kept as records. **This is called records management.**

- Ascertains the categories of data that belong in the records category.
- Identifies the appropriate handling and collection procedures for current documents that will be declared records, as well as how they should be treated while they are being utilized.
- Determines the appropriate retention period and method for each kind of record to comply with legal, commercial, or regulatory obligations.
- Looks into and puts into practice business procedures and technology solutions to assist make sure the company complies with its records management requirements economically and unobtrusively.
- Completes responsibilities pertaining to records, such as finding and preserving documents connected to outside events like litigation or getting rid of outdated records.

Corporate compliance officers, records managers, and lawyers are in charge of figuring out which papers and other real or digital things in your company are records. These people can help you make sure that papers are kept for the right amount of time by carefully organizing all of your company's business content. Legal protection, regulatory compliance, and increased organizational speed are all benefits of a well-designed records management system. This is because it encourages the proper disposal of old items that are not records.

A records management system includes the following elements:

- **A content analysis** that lists and organizes content in the business that can be turned into records, as well as the content's source places and the steps it will take to get to the records management application.
- There should be **a file plan** that lists where each type of business record should be kept, the rules that apply, how long it should be kept, how it should be thrown away, and who is in charge of handling it.
- **A document outlining compliance standards** that outlines the guidelines that the company's IT systems must adhere to to guarantee compliance as well as the procedures used to guarantee enterprise team members' involvement
- **A way to gather files and records that are no longer being used** from all record sources, like email systems, collaboration servers, and file servers.

- **A way to check records** while they are still being used.
- **A way to keep track of the metadata** and check logs of records.
- **A way to keep records** (put off destroying them) whiles certain things happen, like lawsuits.
- **A way to keep an eye on and report on how records** are being handled to make sure that workers are following the rules and following the policies when they file, view, and manage records.

SharePoint has features that can help businesses set up systems and methods for managing records that work together.

Overview of records management planning

This topic talks about the steps you should take during planning to help you be sure that the SharePoint-based records management system you set up will help your company reach its records management goals.

Here's an overview of the planning process for records management:

1. Identify records management roles: For records management to work well, there need to be specific people in charge, like records managers and compliance officers, who organize the organization's data and run the process of records management.
- IT staff to set up the tools that make record-keeping work well.
- Content managers need to know where the company's records are kept and make sure that their teams follow the rules for managing records.

2. Analyze organizational content: Before making a file plan, content managers and records managers look at how papers are used in the company to see which ones can be turned into records.

3. Make a file plan. Fill in the rest of the file plan after you have looked at the content of your group and decided how long to keep things. While file plans are different from one company to the next, in general, they list the types of things that the company considers to be records, where they are kept, how long they are kept, and other details like who is in charge of them and what larger group of records they are a part of.

4. Develop retention schedules. For each type of record, figure out when it is no longer active (being used), how long it should be kept after that, and how it should be thrown away at the end.

5. Evaluate and improve document management practices. Also, make sure that the right rules are being followed in places where documents are kept. For instance, make sure that the information is being reviewed correctly so that the right reports are kept with the records.

6. Design the records management solution: Choose whether to make a backup for records, handle records as they are now, or use a mix of the two. Design the record collection based on your file plan, or figure out how to use current sites to store records. Set up content types, libraries, rules, and, if needed, information that tells the system where to send a document.

7. Plan how content turns into records: If you use SharePoint for both active document management and records management, you can make your processes move documents to a library for records. If you use SharePoint or an outside document management system, you can plan and build links that move content from those systems to the records folder or that mark a document as a record but don't move it. You also make a plan for how users will learn how to make records and work with them.

8. **Plan email integration**. Choose whether you will handle your email records in SharePoint or in the email tool itself.

9. **Plan compliance for social content**. If your company uses blogs, wikis or other social media, figure out how this content will be turned into records.

10. **Plan compliance reporting and documentation**. You should write down your records management plans and processes to make sure your organization is following the rules for records management and to let others know about these rules. For example, if your company is sued over records, you may need to show these records management rules, execution plans, and success data.

Overview of SharePoint Record Centers

We can say that the process of automatically storing old documents in one place is called record archiving, and it is handled by the record center site collection. It can be used in many ways. The first way is as a central place to store documents. For instance, if you have a lot of documents in the active document library, it might get too full after a few days, which could cause the well-known SharePoint list view threshold error. The old documents need to be moved to a different site, which is just a document center, to prevent this from happening. If certain conditions in the content type IRM (Information Right Management) policy are met, the document will be moved to the record center site. I will talk more about this in the next section. You could also use it if you want to manage all of your documents from one place. For example, if you have a legal document, a sales order document, a purchase order document, a finance document, a sales document, and so on, you might want to upload them all to one place and have them automatically routed to the appropriate sites. You can do this by configuring content organizer rules in the record center site.

Note:

- Once a document is in the record library, it is locked and can't be deleted. This is done automatically by the record center.
- We can even make a document a record on the team site, but we need to set up a workflow or use Power Automate to do it.
- The record stage of a document's lifecycle is the last one, so it gets locked.

We now have a good idea of what a SharePoint Online record center is and why we need one. We will now talk about how to set up the archiving system.

How to configure the record center archiving mechanism in SharePoint Online?

There are three steps to setting up the record center in SharePoint Online:

- Put together a record center site collection
- Set up the connection to the record center in Microsoft 365 Record Center;
- Make and set up the content organizer rule in the record center site collection.

I made the record center site collection below as part of the demo.

- Visit the **site's settings** page.
- Click on "**Content organizer settings**" in the **Site Administration** section.
- Then we will arrive at the page where we can configure the Content organizer settings.
- At the very bottom of this page, we can see the URL for the web service that was submitted.

Note down the web service URL:

- *https://globalsharepoint2020.sharepoint.com/sites/TestRecordCenter/_vti_bin/OfficialFile.asmx*

As we set up the connection to the record center in the Microsoft 365 admin center, we will need this web service URL. Please remember this.

Duplicate Submissions

Specify what should occur when a file with the same name already exists in a target location.

If versioning is not enabled in a target library, the organizer will append unique characters to duplicate submissions regardless of the setting selected here.

○ Use SharePoint versioning.
● Append unique characters to the end of duplicate filenames

Preserving Context

The organizer can save the original audit logs and properties if they are included with submissions. The saved logs and properties are stored in an audit entry on the submitted document.

☑ Save the original audit log and properties of submitted content

Rule Managers

Specify the users who manage the rules and can respond when incoming content doesn't match any rule.

Rule Managers must have the Manage Web Site permission to access the content organizer rules list from the site settings page.

☑ E-mail rule managers when submissions do not match a rule
☑ E-mail rule managers when content has been left in the Drop Off Library
Enter users or groups separated by semicolons:

SHAREPOINT\system

No exact match was found. Click the item(s) that did not resolve for more options.

Number of days to wait before sending an e-mail: 3

Submission Points

Use this information to set up other sites or e-mail messaging software to send content to this site.

Web service URL: https://globalsharepoint2020.sharepoint.com/sites/TestRecordCenter/_vti_bin/OfficialFile.asmx
E-mail address:

132

CHAPTER 12
SHAREPOINT DEVELOPMENT AND EXTENSIBILITY

Introduction to SharePoint Development

SharePoint is a flexible development tool that can be used to make client-side parts, add-ins, and solutions that cover a wide range of needs. The SharePoint developer manual walks you through the platform's features, technologies, options, and ways of building apps that make it unique as a development tool. One of the best things about SharePoint development is how flexible it is. It gives developers a way to make solutions that meet a wide range of business needs. SharePoint supports many ways of building apps, such as using SharePoint Designer for no-code solutions, Power Platform for low-code solutions, and standard server-side development with languages like **C# and ASP.NET**.

There are two main types of SharePoint development: frontend development and server development. Frontend development uses tools like HTML, CSS, and JavaScript to make applications that look good and are easy to use. Developers use SharePoint's client-side object model (CSOM) and SharePoint Framework (SPFx) to make the experience better for users and make web parts that are dynamic and engaging. Backend development, on the other hand, is all about reasoning and data handling on the server side. To make their own web parts, processes, and event handlers, developers use languages like C# and tools like Visual Studio. The powerful API set in SharePoint lets developers work with the platform's data, which makes it easy to connect to other services and systems.

SharePoint Framework (SPFx) for Modern Sites

The SharePoint Framework (SPFx) is a page and web part model that lets you build SharePoint on the client side, easily connect to SharePoint data, and add features to Microsoft Teams and Microsoft Viva. You can use current web technologies and tools in your favorite programming environment with the SharePoint Framework to make useful experiences and apps that work on any device. The SPFx approach is the best way for developers to customize and add to SharePoint. Since SharePoint Online, Microsoft Teams, and Microsoft Viva Connections all work hand-in-hand, developers can use SPFx to make all of these tools more flexible and useful. The SPFx is the only option for Viva Connections' extension and customization. You only need to write the code once, and it will be used in many different apps. The picture below shows an example case that has a standard answer on GitHub.

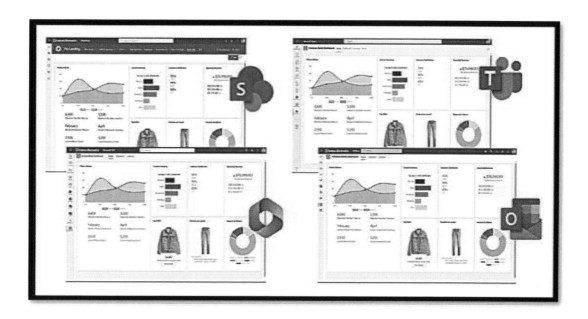

You can build your own Adaptive Card Extensions with SPFx to add to Microsoft Viva Connections.

CHAPTER 13
MIGRATION STRATEGIES AND BEST PRACTICES
Planning a SharePoint Migration

It makes sense that a lot of companies move to SharePoint because it is the best cloud option for groups that want to store, share, and work together on material in one safe place. SharePoint makes it easy for businesses to share information, which helps every project team, department, and division work together. Many companies choose it because of its high degree of customization and ease of internal and external collaboration on PC and mobile devices. Companies can send out personalized, focused news through SharePoint to keep their workers updated and improve the efficiency of the company. On top of that, SharePoint has a strong search function that helps users find information and ideas that can help them make decisions. SharePoint changes the way businesses work and makes them more productive by giving customers a rich digital experience. This is why more than 200,000 companies use it for their intranets, team sites, and content management.

The Importance of a SharePoint Migration Plan

Moving software can be hard, so it's important to make a plan to make sure it goes smoothly and no important things get lost. You need to make sure that your team still has everything they need to do their jobs and doesn't run into any problems during or after the move.

To make the process easier, we've put together a list of step-by-step steps that will make the move to SharePoint for your company easier. We'll talk about these below.

The Steps Involved in a SharePoint Migration

1. Think about the future and goals of your business.
Think about what your business is trying to do and where it wants to go. Think about how plans for project management and reorganizing the company might impact the flow of information and the transfer process. Check to see if now is a good time to move to SharePoint.

2. Put together a migration team.
Creating a team to manage the transfer process is one way to make sure it goes smoothly. Another option is to hire an outside team of SharePoint experts who can help with planning, audits, paperwork, and testing.

3. Analyze your existing content and organization.
View and examine the information about the content you want to move to SharePoint again. Some of the information may be out of date and no longer useful to your business. It can save you time during the transfer process to delete or archive this information.

4. Set up your new environment.

When setting up your new surroundings, make sure to focus on getting the best results possible. At this point, does it make sense to change how some information is organized? Or, would it be better to keep things as close as possible to how they are now? Set up your new space so that users can find material quickly and easily.

5. Migrate to SharePoint.

Your migration team can start moving once your new setup is set up. We suggest that you migrate in one of two ways: 1) in stages so that you can communicate with people well, or 2) all at once to keep things simple. One way might work better than the other depending on your people.

6. Conduct testing.

Last but not least, try everything to make sure it works the way it should. Experts in data migration are very helpful at this step because they know what to look for and can make sure that all the data has been moved correctly. You can make sure that the migration to SharePoint goes smoothly and that everyone in your organization has a better experience by doing these things.

Executing a Smooth Migration Process

You should now think about the real migration since you have a plan in place. For your SharePoint migration to go smoothly, you need to take four more steps:

1) Governance and Clean Up
2) Test Migration
3) Migration
4) Decommissioning

SharePoint Migration Step 1: Governance & Clean-Up

Before you move from one file share or even SharePoint site to another, you should make sure you know the rules for the new site so you don't bring any old junk with you. In this part of the migration plan, you should organize your files, choose the tags you'll use to group them, get rid of any extra copies of files on your current system, and set up rules for how your new system will work.

SharePoint Migration Step 2: Test Migration

In this part of the migration plan, you test the migration on your SharePoint site before you do the real migration. There are a lot of limits on how you can work with data on Office 365, which makes migrations hard. It's important to test because file names can only have a certain number of characters and can't be too long. File paths can also only have a certain number of characters, and so on. You should use the right test tools to make sure that everything will move over correctly.

SharePoint Migration Step 3: Migration

The real migration of your information to your new SharePoint site can begin after the testing is complete. Your SharePoint migration will proceed in the manner you choose at this point. You might only want to move ten people or a department at first. If possible, move the servers one at a time. You decide how to get rid of your old system.

SharePoint Migration Step 4: Decommissioning

It's time to shut down your old site once you're done with your SharePoint migration. Again, this can be done in stages: turn off each server one at a time, decommission ten people at a time, or use another plan.

CHAPTER 14
SHAREPOINT FOR ENTERPRISE SOLUTIONS
Scaling SharePoint for Enterprise Deployments

You want to get that new SharePoint-based site up and running as soon as possible after all the work you put into it. But what would be the best way to do that?

Note: This advice is mostly for SharePoint Online, but most of it also works for websites hosted in a SharePoint system that is on-premises.

What not to do

Here is a list of the most important things you should not do when setting up your platform.

Don't:
- Put your gateway through a lot of stress tests against your SharePoint Online user.
- Do a **"big bang release,"** which means letting all of your customers see your new page at the same time.
- Let a lot of security groups join your site group so that everyone can use your page. A lot of security groups (30–40,000) can be affected by this, but each one can only belong to one site group. Or, fewer security groups can be affected by this and belong to many site groups.

How you did this in the past

When SharePoint was still on-premises, customers would often put their sites through huge stress tests to see if the system could handle the load and still allow pages to load quickly.

But you can't do a traditional stress test with SharePoint Online because:

- SharePoint Online sees the load test as a denial-of-service attack and blocks the user or, even worse, the whole tenant;
- If the load test isn't blocked, it's slowed down, which makes the test results hard to understand;
- SharePoint Online dynamically scales its infrastructure, which is great, but not if you suddenly do a huge load in. The back-end model that scales needs time to adjust to the extra work.
- This kind of speed test only checks for errors once, but your portal will change over time. It's better to use the built-in portal statistics so that you can keep an eye on how well your portal is doing. To make a load test that shows how the system is used is also hard.

Using a staged roll-out plan and built-in portal data to track portal performance as more users are added is the best way to get your new portal up and running. More information about this method is given in the next part.

Use a phased roll-out plan and telemetry

If you want to add new features, you should use a staged method, which usually includes the following:

- **A pilot wave**: The portal is now open to a small group of key users for the first time. It's important to get a group of reps, or vital, key users who can give you the first feedback.
- **One or more end-user waves**: If you're following a certain plan, the number of waves you have will depend on how many people you have. Some companies set their roll-out steps based on how their business is set up, while others set them based on country or area. Finally, the most important thing is that you're slowly adding new people to the site.

A plan for a slow roll-out is shown in the next figure. Keep in mind that this accounts for the fact that end-user waves usually have fewer busy users than invited-user waves.

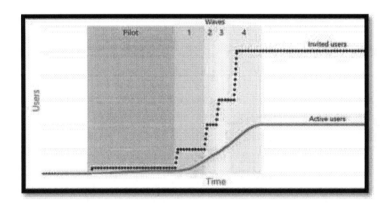

This step-by-step process gives you time to think about the feedback you're getting and make any necessary changes to your site. But how do you track and measure success during this phased roll-out? Adding site data to your application is the best way to go about this. Getting performance info on the site all the time helps you figure out if the speed changes as the number of people hikes. This can also be useful when you change the site in the future.

Successful Intranet Portal with SharePoint

Intranet portals are at the top of the list for business collaboration. For their collaboration needs, more and more companies are turning to the intranet. It is also a market that is rising. According to Statista, the market for collaboration software will continue to grow and bring in about 13.58 billion US dollars in 2023. These numbers show how much money companies spend on a variety of collaboration tools. The intranet site will probably be the most expensive item on this list because it is used by more workers of all ages. Microsoft SharePoint is at the top of the list of the best websites on the market. Microsoft first released SharePoint in 2001. Since then, it has gone through many changes and updates that have made it the most popular choice for businesses looking for a collaboration tool. For almost 20 years, SharePoint has consistently been the most popular collaboration tool. What's so great about SharePoint? First, there's how easy it is to use. SharePoint is very simple to set up and handle, and because it's so flexible, it fits the needs of any business precisely. Another good thing about SharePoint is that it's simple to set up and businesses can trust the service quality.

Why should companies adopt a SharePoint Intranet Portal?

There are many collaboration tools on the market today that businesses can buy to help their employees work together. But why should they choose an intranet? The only thing that makes an intranet site stand out is that it can hold all of the collaboration tools in a single place. By putting it all together, companies can keep information consistent, make sure that knowledge is shared centrally, and support a unified communication environment. The users can also gain from this because the unified information store makes it easy for them to find and use the information. An intranet gateway cuts down on the number of clicks a user needs to make to get to a piece of information. Here are some more things that an intranet site can do.

- An intranet can interact on many levels. Businesses will have many departments, and it should be easy for people from different departments to speak with one another. Intranet sites make this possible.
- Content management is one of the most important features of an intranet. The intranet will be the central place where you can store and access documents.
- With an intranet, it's easy to manage collaboration between departments and teams.
- Intranets are the safest way to create an integrated collaborative environment.

There are many intranet gateway options on the market, but SharePoint is the best one. Let's find out the reason for that. The best thing about SharePoint is that it can be changed to fit your needs. SharePoint comes with a lot of web parts, and you can even add your own to make it even better. These groups can use these to make their web portals that they can use. It is this ability to change or adapt that makes a SharePoint intranet site into a full business system that can handle many functions. In these areas, you might find anything from an HR management system to a simple document management system.

SharePoint Intranet Development

SharePoint has been around for 20 years and has been the best software on the market. It has also changed a lot over that time. What's more, Microsoft keeps adding to SharePoint every day to make it a better intranet platform. **The SharePoint intranet can have four different builds, depending on which versions Microsoft makes public.**

1. SharePoint Intranet On-Premises Solution
2. SharePoint Online (Stand-alone)
3. SharePoint Online (part of O365)
4. SharePoint Online (Part of M365)

When you are building a SharePoint community, you need to think about what you want to get out of it. Here are some works requirements that the intranet needs to meet. **'My Site**,' which is an employee's area with work-related details and the projects they are working on, can be set up for this in on-premise versions. It should include their work. In Office 365 versions, you can view an employee's biography in Delve to see what they are working on, who they are interacting with, etc. You can now use Microsoft Delve for this. You should also add a way for teams to work together on the website. The **"Team Sites"** feature of SharePoint makes this possible. This is where teams can store and view papers, share ideas, and talk about what's going on. Team sites are very simple to set up and adjust. Even someone who doesn't know much about SharePoint can make simple changes to the site. You can also make changes to these pages with the web parts that come with SharePoint. It's easy for site owners to control who can see and change the information on these pages, as well as who can just read them.

'Communication Sites' lets you make teams' websites look much better. It has lots of cool features, like the Hero Web part, which is a content slider where you can add pictures and videos. Like Teams, communication sites can be changed in any way you want. Another great thing about SharePoint Online right now is that it has a feature called **"Hub Sites**." These sites bring together information from different linked sites, like Team sites and Communication sites. It's like the home page for your community. A business wiki, blogs, community sites, community platforms, and project sites are just a few of the other types of sites that SharePoint offers to improve team collaboration. Using these tools, you need to make a collaboration site that works for your teams, meets user needs, and makes the job of workers easier. By improving the collaboration process, you can increase the team's output. For a better collaboration experience, you can always ask SharePoint pros to create and build your team sites.

SharePoint Intranet for Enterprise Collaboration

The only goal of enterprise collaboration is to make it easy and quick for all users to get information. With SharePoint Intranet, you can use personalized web parts on the site to show information from across the whole company. Since it will be the home page for the company's intranet, you should put a lot of thought into how it looks. The top page should have all the news about what the group is doing, important links, and ways to get to important papers and other information. A company can use the SharePoint intranet's useful features. *Project Management Solutions, Contract Management, Document Management, Asset Management, HR Management*, and many more are some of these features.

Intranet Management

It is important to properly handle an intranet once your company has chosen one. You should keep the material up to date and make it more engaging so that people use the solution. Concerning user uptake, teach users how to use the website, show new features, and get regular comments from them. Organizations spend a lot of time and money improving their intranet but don't bother getting people to use it. As a result, the intranet isn't used and the company loses a lot of money. You need to keep an eye on the solution and give it regular upkeep. Lastly, you need to keep the answer up to date with any new features or bug fixes. These updates don't have to be big changes. Updating the system and making sure it is safe are important parts of handling the intranet. All of these perquisites come from SharePoint Intranets. Think about them before you decide.

CHAPTER 15

MOBILE ACCESS AND RESPONSIVE DESIGN

Accessing SharePoint on Mobile Devices

Use your cell phone to stay in touch with your coworkers and work. If you want to connect to your SharePoint site without using a web browser, you can download the SharePoint app for Apple iOS or Android.

What's possible?

Use your mobile phone or tablet to:

- **Find SharePoint Sites**. This will show you a list of sites that you have been following on Microsoft SharePoint Online or that the administrators have told you about.
- **Changing site views**: In SharePoint Online, you can see some of your sites and libraries by switching between the full-screen view (also called the PC view) and the mobile view. It is best to use the PC View for better speed, especially when adding custom CSS to your sites.
- **Document Management**: Check through the most recent documents, such as MS Word, Excel, PowerPoint, or PDF, that were shared with you and view and share them within SharePoint. Additionally, in Microsoft SharePoint Online, you can view the papers you are watching.
- **Navigation**: Use the menus to go from one site to Microsoft OneDrive for Business or from one site to another.

Let us check out how SharePoint Online functions on both a mobile browser and a mobile app:

SharePoint Mobile Browser Interface

Open and browse a SharePoint site

Open a SharePoint site

1. Use your phone to open the online browser.
2. Type the website address (URL) for SharePoint Online into the address bar.
3. Take **mydock365 SharePoint** as an example. Instead of mydock365, your URL will have your domain name.
4. Use your work or school account to log in.
5. Click on Go in the bottom left area of the screen. It's possible that you need to tap the down arrow **(...)** to see the Go to button.
6. Pick **Sites** from the list of tiles that let you move around.

You'll see a list of SharePoint sites grouped into two groups: sites I'm watching and sites that have been promoted. **Sites I'm following** are more like a list of all the sites you visit.

Browsing a SharePoint site

- On the Sites page, select the site that you want to view from the **Sites I'm following** or **Promoted sites.** Apps are where document files and lists are kept, and Subsites are where any subsites are kept.

You can tell which site you're watching by looking at the name of the view at the top of the page.

- Click on the tile **Site Assets** to view a site's OneNote notebook.
- Choose the document library that has the file you want to see to view it on your site.

Opening your OneDrive for Business document library

1. If you are already logged in to a SharePoint site on your computer, tap Go in the bottom left corner of the screen and choose OneDrive. It should open OneDrive for Business.

2. If you aren't already logged in to a SharePoint site, open your app's web browser and do these steps:
- Type the website address (URL) for SharePoint Online into the address bar. Take http://mydock365.sharepoint.com as an example. Instead of Contoso, your URL will have your domain name.
- Use your work or school account to sign in, like joe@mydock365.onmicrosoft.com.
- Click on Go in the bottom left area of the screen. It's possible that you need to tap the down arrow (...) to see the Go to button.
- Pick **OneDrive** from the list of tiles.

How to switch between mobile and full-screen view

You can see your SharePoint sites and OneDrive for Business library in phone view or PC view, which is the full-size view.

Switch from mobile view to PC view

1. Press the "More" button in the bottom right area of a site or library.
2. Pick "**Switch to PC view**."

Switch from PC view to mobile view

1. Go to the SharePoint site and click on **Settings** in the upper right part of the screen.
Setting may not show up if you are in full-screen view. In the top right corner of your screen, next to Edit, tap the **Focus on Content** button.
2. Pick "**Mobile view**" from the Tools menu.

SharePoint Mobile App Interface

Are you sick of using URLs every time to log in to SharePoint? With the SharePoint app, you can get to your intranet with just a touch. It's especially helpful for sales teams that are always on the go because SharePoint helps them stay up to date on papers, team sites, company platforms, and other users who work together. View and update the SharePoint lists on your SharePoint Team Sites, as well as take a look at the site actions and quickly access the most-used or most recent documents. You need to log in to your SharePoint Online account. You can add more than one account and quickly switch between them.

Note: For this to work, your company must already have a current Office 365 plan that includes SharePoint Online.

SharePoint Mobile App: Login Screen and News Feed Interface

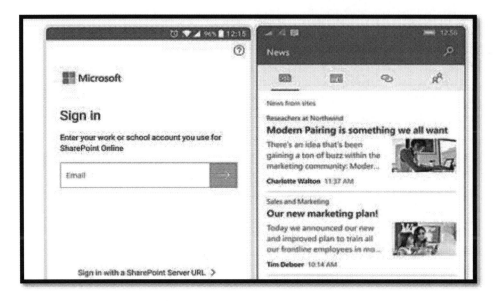

The Search interface in the SharePoint App

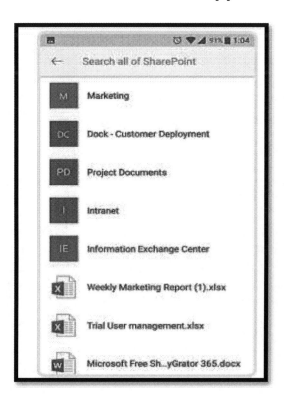

The mobile app has **Enterprise Search** built in, and the results are sorted into files, sites, and people, as shown above.

The Links Tab in the SharePoint Mobile App

The picture shows the Links tab. This is where you can find advertising links for your business. Your SharePoint Administrator is in charge of this for your workers, and these links will help you find information on the company sites and tools you want.

Supporting the SharePoint mobile apps online and on-premises

Your SharePoint users can use the SharePoint mobile app for iOS, Android, and Windows Mobile to work on their files and data while on the go. When you are in charge of an on-premises SharePoint Server farm, you need to know these rules.

You can use the SharePoint mobile app to:

- Get to and work on your sites in SharePoint in Microsoft 365;
- The SharePoint mobile app works best for people working on intranet sites while connected to a business network. This is true whether your SharePoint setting is on-premises or on an iOS or Android device.

Common messages received by users

When your users or you log in to the SharePoint mobile app, they may see information about the type of SSL or TLS certificate or login method being used. These messages let users and managers know about ways to join SharePoint that are allowed.

The following are some of the most popular words and what they mean:

- **This app doesn't work with the unverified SSL certificate that the SharePoint Server is using**. The SharePoint mobile app also can't use self-signed certificates or certificates given by an in-house Certificate Authority (CA). An SSL or TLS certificate from a public Certificate Authority is what you'll need to secure your SharePoint web apps.
- **SharePoint Server uses basic authentication, which this app doesn't support yet**. The SharePoint mobile app, on the other hand, can use NTLM security and Forms-based identity.

Is this network traffic from the SharePoint mobile app?

Administrators may see strange data on their network monitors when iOS and Android devices are linked to SharePoint Server 2016 (on-premises). Internet users may see query and question-response traffic going to and from sites like *bl3301-g.1drv.com, bn2.vortex.data.microsoft.com.akadns.net*, or even *weu-breeziest-in.cloudapp.net*. These calls have to do with tracking services and gathering data. For analytics reasons, telemetry data is used to keep an eye on how Microsoft 365 customers use the services and to get basic information about how reliable the services are. As an example, the first URL given, bl3301-g.1drv.com, is for OneDrive, and a lot of the other URLs will have Microsoft in the domain name. Administrators should be notified of any strange network data and look into it. Make sure you know that you can't turn off the data collection and tracking services for the SharePoint mobile app while you do this. If you want to know if the SharePoint mobile app is right for your business, reading the Privacy Statements can help.

CHAPTER 16
DISASTER RECOVERY AND BACKUP STRATEGIES

Understanding SharePoint Backup

Any business needs to back up SharePoint; it's important! Safeguarding your data and getting it back in case something goes wrong. There are several ways to back up: SharePoint's tool, third-party tools, or doing it by hand. The SharePoint farm, files, and settings must all be backed up completely before the process can begin. A good backup plan keeps your business going and stops you from losing info. When making a plan, you should think about how often, what kind of backup (full or partial), where to store the data, and how long to keep it. Always check your copies to make sure they are correct. If you need to, you can talk to a professional because the basic way might not fully back up some features. It was said by Forbes that 60% of small businesses that lose their data shut down within six months. Plan and carry out the SharePoint backup strategy to keep the business running smoothly. Don't worry about losing your SharePoint info; give it some love and backup.

Different Methods to Protect Your SharePoint Data

Your SharePoint data will be safe and sound as long as you use backup methods. Here are some tried-and-true ways to keep your SharePoint setting safe.

- **Full Back-up**: This option saves all of the site's material, along with its settings and permissions, to a backup file.
- **Differential Backup**: Keeps track of all the changes that have been made since the last full backup.
- **Incremental Backup**: This type of backup keeps track of changes made to site collections since the last full or partial backup.
- **Granular Backup**: This type of backup only protects certain SharePoint sites, lists, or document stores.

You can also back up your SharePoint data with third-party tools like CloudAlly, Veeam, and AvePoint or you can use the tools that come with SharePoint. It is important to try the backup and recovery process regularly to make sure that the saved files can be accessed and used in an emergency.

Full Farm Backup

SharePoint is ideal for team collaboration and data handling. Back up your SharePoint info often to keep it safe.

You can choose the "Full Farm Backup" option. To:

- Go to the site for the Central Administration. Pick "**Backup and Restore**."
- Click "**Start Backup**" after choosing "**Farm Backup**."
- Choose a place to keep the backup file.
- Check your settings. Click on "**Back Up Now**."

Be Patient, because Full Farm Backup takes time. You're done with the backup after these steps. Schedule backups for times when there isn't much going on, like when you're not working. To make things safer, save the backup copy somewhere else. SharePoint Health Analyzer is being used to keep an eye out for any problems or alerts. Your SharePoint info will be safe if you do this. Granular backup takes a lot of time, but it's worth it in the end.

Granular Backup

For SharePoint to work, granular backup is a must. It keeps data safe and saves time and space. Users can use PowerShell or Central Admin, which are built into SharePoint, to do this. You can also use third-party backup tools that are easier for regular people to use. You can back up individual lists, books, sites, and even papers with granular backup. Customized rules and plans can make it run itself. It makes it less likely that data will be lost. Plus, cloud-based services like Microsoft 365 give you the tools to make very detailed backups.

Pro Tip: Make sure you test your backups often. It will ensure that things will be fixed in a situation.

Backup via PowerShell

Want to save a copy of your SharePoint data? PowerShell from Microsoft is the answer! This tool is strong and flexible, and it has a command-line interface for quick tasks. **Let us look at the steps for using PowerShell to make a good backup.**

1. Run "***Add-PSSnapin Microsoft.SharePoint.Powershell***" in Windows PowerShell to login to SharePoint.
2. Pick out the site group or subsite that you want to save. "***New-Item E:\Backup -type directory***" will make a new folder for backups.
3. Use cmdlets like ***Backup-SPFarm, Backup-SPConfigurationDatabase, or Export-SPWeb*** to make a new backup object.
4. Pick the type of backup you want to use—full or split.
5. Type "***Backup-SPFarm -Directory E:\Backup -BackupMethod Full***" to begin the backup process.

Steps 2, 3, 4, and 5 must be done again if you want to back up more than one subsite or collection of sites. PowerShell makes it easy to keep an eye on backups of SharePoint data while keeping them small so they are easy to store and get. These steps help you feel safe and save time in case of an emergency. Don't let bad things happen to Simple Things Publishing; use PowerShell to back up SharePoint today!

Third-Party Backup Solutions

Third-party backup options may have features that aren't available in backup tools that come with SharePoint. With these options, you can back up and recover everything, and you can also make backups of specific files or parts of files. There are also options for automated schedule and reporting, as well as more thorough data on the state and performance of backups. When picking a third-party backup option, think about how easy it is to use, how scalable it is, and how well it works with other systems. You can choose from Commvault Complete Backup & Recovery for SharePoint, Veeam Backup & Replication for Microsoft SharePoint and Druva inSync for SharePoint. Overall, these advanced features keep your SharePoint data safe from being deleted by accident or lost in other ways. Do not forget to back up your SharePoint. It's like having your ex's phone number on hand in case you need it.

Best Practices for SharePoint Backup

Keeping backups of SharePoint info is very important for keeping the business running. Best Practices for SharePoint Backup are needed for backup and emergency recovery strategies. **This is what we think about SharePoint Backup:**

- Make sure you have a backup plan so that backups happen regularly.
- *Use incremental backups* instead of full backups to cut down on backup time and size;
- Run a restore job on the backup data to make sure the backups are correct;
- *Store multiple copies of backups* in different places to lower the risk of losing data;
- Set up security protocols to keep people from getting in without permission and encrypt backups for privacy;

SharePoint Backup has its twists and turns, like how to handle lost data and deleted sites. It's important to fully grasp these changes if you want to make SharePoint Backup rules that work well and are useful.

Determine Backup Frequency

It's important to back up your SharePoint data in case of disasters, system failure, or deletion by mistake. **Based on the value of your data and how frequently it changes, determine how frequently you need to backup.**

- **Daily Backups**—it's best to back up every day if changes are made every day.
- **Weekly Backups**: Weekly backups are adequate for info that doesn't change very often.
- **Monthly Backups**: Monthly backups can save time and room for data that doesn't change often.

- **Quarterly/Half-Yearly/Yearly Backups**: Less-used data can be backed up every three, six, or twelve months for legal reasons or storage.

Keep more than one copy of your backup offline in case of fires, storms, or other natural disasters. Verify that the backup service can bring back all of SharePoint's content, not just certain files.

Store Backups Securely

Keeping backups in a safe place is important for keeping your SharePoint system safe and working right. Two important ways to do this are to encrypt files and keep them in a safe place. Role-based access control can be used to add extra protection by only letting people who are supposed to be there in. Having multiple copies saved in different safe sites is advised to protect against data loss from tech failure or disasters. Also, trying the backup method often makes sure it will work right when it's needed. If you follow these best practices for SharePoint backup storage, you can be sure that no one else can get to your data without your permission and that it is safe in case something unexpected happens. Things that back up and recover are like relationships: you won't know if they work until it's too late.

Test Backup and Restore Processes

For data access and dependability, you must test your backup and recovery methods. Use this as a guide:

- Make a copy of your real setting in the test environment.
- Make fake data to test with.
- Take a full backup of the test place.
- Get rid of one or more fake sets.
- Get back the lost info from the full backup.
- Make sure the returned data works by trying how it works.

Don't think that your backups worked just because they were done. Include and test your emergency rescue plans. Do regular tests, such as drills that aren't planned. Get ready for bad things to happen because you never know when they will. In this case, a company was shocked when its server crashed. Some of the files they tried to restore from backups were damaged or lost, so they failed. Instead of doing important work, they fixed old files for hours. This could have been avoided by testing often. Backing up SharePoint configurations is like wearing a helmet while riding a bike: it's uncomfortable, but you have to do it to avoid a crash.

Backup SharePoint Configuration

Backing up your SharePoint config files is a must for smooth operation.

Here's how to do it!

- Click on Administrative Tools in the Start Menu and then click on SharePoint Central Administration.
- From the menu on the left, choose "**Backup and Restore**." Then, hit "**Perform a backup**."
- Select "**Farm Backup**" on the "**Backup Options**" page. In Farm Selection, choose all of the parts. Choose "**Full**" for the Type and a backup plan.

To keep data from getting lost, it's very important to keep backup methods up to date.

A *Pro Tip*: Give each backup its name so you don't accidentally delete another one.

Restoring SharePoint from Backup

Because of how much we depend on technology these days, all businesses must back up their info. SharePoint, a popular tool for document management and collaboration, is included. In the event of data loss or damage that wasn't expected, quickly recovering backed-up data becomes very important. This is how you can get back to SharePoint from a backup.

These six easy steps will bring back SharePoint from a backup:

- Open SharePoint Central Administration on the server where the backup was made to begin.
- Go to **Backup and Restore**, click on **Restore from Backup**, and then find the backup file.
- Pick a healing point and pick the site group you want to bring back.
- Pick the parts of the backup that you want to recover, like lists, libraries, and permissions.
- Choose the repair options, such as "**overwrite file**" and "**create new sites**."
- To finish the repair process, click **OK**.

It's important to regularly back up your SharePoint data and the parts that are linked to it. Adding an emergency recovery plan for the company is another step to think about. This kind of plan can include having an off-site data storing option, checking files for accuracy, and backing up and trying emergency recovery plans right away. Updating and checking files regularly, even on days with little action, is the only way to make sure that the SharePoint restore process works. A backup and emergency recovery option that is based in the cloud is worth looking into because it is more flexible and easier to access. Lastly, use standard security measures in the business to protect the backup data from threats like online threats. Remember that while there's no place like home, there's also no place like an up-to-date backup if you need to recover SharePoint from a full-farm backup.

Restore from Full Farm Backup

It is important to keep the security of your data, so follow these four steps to recover SharePoint from a Full Farm Backup:

- Make sure you have the accounts and permissions you need.

- Select "**Backup and Restore**" from the System Settings menu in Central Administration.
- Click "**Restore from Backup**" and find the file that has a full backup of your farm.
- Pick which parts to restore, make sure the settings are correct, and start the recovery.

Keep in mind that this might take a while, based on how many files you have. Check and test backups regularly so that you are ready when you need to be. Restoring from a backup should be done before trying to fix damaged data. The SharePoint literature says that this method can be used to restore a farm to its original state after a disaster. But partial backup can bring SharePoint back to life like a zombie bug!

Restore from Granular Backup

There are three steps to recover from Granular Backup for SharePoint:

- Find the group of sites and go to the backup folder.
- Move the site files to where they belong in SharePoint.
- Do a full search of the source of the information.

Don't forget to check that item-level restores won't delete features that are already there. Granular saves give you options. They can get back some info and items without messing up the rest. In this way, admins can get lists or papers back if they were wiped by accident.

Restore via PowerShell

To quickly restore SharePoint from a backup, you can use PowerShell. It takes a lot of skill, but it makes sure that all of your info and settings are returned. How to do it:

- Log in as an administrator to the SharePoint Management Shell.
- Type the following: **Restore-SPFarm -Directory <Path to Backup Folder> -RestoreMethod Overwrite -Item** Restore Type'. 'Restore Type' could be an online app, content database, or group of sites.
- Hit "**Enter**" and wait for the repair to finish.

You need to be able to get to the target place and have enough disk space. Based on the size of the backup, the amount of free room, and the location of the disk, each restore has its own needs. In a hurry, a senior worker once used PowerShell to bring back a database that had an important document library. After two hours, he was thrilled that nothing had gone wrong and no data had been lost or damaged. He now has even more faith that PowerShell is a great tool for SharePoint managers. If you need to restore SharePoint from a third-party backup, it's like having a superhero at your disposal. You don't always need them, but when you do, they're lifesavers.

Restore Using Third-Party Backup Solutions

Third-party tools can be used to restore SharePoint from a backup. These options add an extra layer of security to help keep your info safe. Here are six steps to follow:

- Choose the best backup service for your SharePoint system that is not built by Microsoft.
- Check to make sure you have a backup of the important files and data.
- Follow the instructions that came with the third-party option to install and set it up.
- Pick the most recent backup version that has the information you require.
- Begin the repair process the way the seller tells you to.
- When you're done, make sure that all of your info is back and test how the system works.

Note: The steps may be different for each seller. So, do what they tell you. Also, be careful when recovering from a backup because if you do it wrong, it could change how the current user experiences the site. **The Worldwide Quarterly Purpose-Built Backup Appliance Tracker from IDC** says that Dell Technologies makes up almost a quarter of the income in the worldwide purpose-built backup market. IT teams stay sane and business data is safe from digital disasters when SharePoint is backed up regularly.

CHAPTER 17

HYBRID DEPLOYMENTS WITH SHAREPOINT SERVER

Integrating SharePoint Online with On-Premises SharePoint Server

Several options are available for combining SharePoint Server on-premises with SharePoint in Microsoft 365. This will make it easier for your users to switch between the two environments. These options can be set up to enhance the user experience during migration from on-premises to the cloud, or they can be used in the long run if you intend to keep using SharePoint Server. Integrating an on-premises SharePoint server with SharePoint Online is a smart move that lets businesses use the best parts of both platforms for a smooth and unified collaboration experience. This connection let's data, content, and services be synced between SharePoint Online in the cloud and SharePoint Server on-premises. This gives users a single platform that makes them more productive and flexible.

When putting this combination into action, there are a few important things to keep in mind and steps to take:

1. **Hybrid Configuration**: SharePoint Hybrid is the official way for Microsoft to connect SharePoint Online and SharePoint Server that is installed on-site. It means making a hybrid system with instances both on-premises and in the cloud. This setup makes it possible for users to have a combined experience, with features like united search, user accounts, and navigation.
2. **Authentication and Identity Management**: You need to take care of authentication and identity management to give users a smooth experience. Azure AD Connect is often set up by organizations to sync their on-premises Active Directory with Azure Active Directory (AAD). This connection makes sure that the names and passwords of users are the same in both settings.
3. **Hybrid Search**: Making sure that all search results are the same is an important part of integration. Users can look for information easily in both on-premises and web settings with a Hybrid look. To do this, a cloud-based search index is set up that includes material from both SharePoint Online and SharePoint Server that is installed on-site.
4. **Integration of OneDrive for Business**: Users can view and work together on their files whether they are saved in SharePoint Online or on-premises when OneDrive for Business is integrated. The end-user experience for file sharing and collaboration is uniform thanks to this interface.
5. **Synchronizing Data:** Some organizations need to share certain data between SharePoint Online and SharePoint Server that is installed on-site. This can include lists, document

files, and other types of information. SharePoint has tools like the SharePoint Migration Tool and SharePoint Content Deployment that make it easier to share data.

6. **Custom Solutions and Workflows**: Any custom solutions, workflows, or third-party interfaces that are used on-premises must be checked to make sure they work with SharePoint Online. Depending on how complicated the current methods are, they may need to be changed or adjusted.

7. **Sharing with others and Security**: Think about the rules and standards for sharing with others and security. SharePoint Online has external sharing features that let users work together with partners from outside the company. Make sure there are security steps in place to control who can access private information from the outside and keep it safe.

8. **Monitoring and Governance**: To handle the linked environment well, set up tracking tools and governance rules. This includes keeping an eye on performance, user behavior, and control rules to make sure security and compliance are always met.

CHAPTER 18
CUSTOMIZING FORMS WITH POWER APPS

Introduction to Power Apps Integration

Users can get a lot out of PowerApps being integrated with SharePoint. It changes how teams work together and deal with data. By joining these two Microsoft platforms without any problems, users can easily access SharePoint data, which allows for real-time changes and makes sure that information is correct.

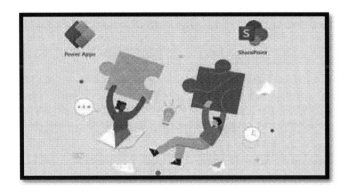

Because PowerApps lets users create interactive forms, they can build and change forms to fit their business needs, which speeds up the data entry process. This connection also makes joint processes easier, which boosts total productivity by letting SharePoint users manage tasks and simplify operations. The main benefit of adding PowerApps is that it gives SharePoint users more control by giving them a set of flexible and useful tools for managing data and working together on projects.

Why integrating PowerApps with SharePoint is essential-

- **PowerApps Available through the SharePoint Mobile App** —People who have downloaded the SharePoint app for Android or iOS can easily use Power Apps from the app. This way, you can keep up with work while you're away from home without having to use your laptop or desktop to get to the Power App on your desktop.
- **SharePoint libraries are accessible**. Power Apps can get a lot of info from a complex library that comes with SharePoint. Once they are integrated, Power Apps can easily get to these libraries, use the data they contain, and make new apps that are uniquely their own. This information can also help business owners and leaders learn more and make decisions.
- **Integrate Power BI**. Power Apps can be used to join SharePoint and Power BI. Because of this, you will be able to see complicated statistics and analytics. They can be added to

your screen so that you can quickly and correctly get the info you need for any business task.

How to integrate PowerApps with SharePoint?

Follow the instructions on the list below to easily connect PowerApps to SharePoint and make your apps:

- Click "**Create**" next to the Power Apps option in the SharePoint list. The computer will open the site creator window when you click on it.
- Since you will know exactly which SharePoint list you want to make the Power App from, it will make the basic version of the app for you.
- If you need to make changes to an app that has already been made, hire a web designer to add features that fit your needs.
- Members of the internal team of the SharePoint lists can then use the apps.
- You can use computer platforms, Windows, Android, and iOS devices to get to the app.

Create a canvas app with data from Microsoft Lists

Here, you'll learn how to use Power Apps to make a canvas app from things in a Microsoft Lists list. The app can be made in either PowerApps for SharePoint Online. If you link to an on-premises SharePoint site through a data connection, you can use Power Apps to make an app based on a list on that site. **There will be three screens in the app you make:**

- You can scroll through the whole list on the browse screen.
- In the details screen, you can see all the facts about a single list item.
- You can make a new thing or change details about a current one in the edit screen.

The ideas and methods here can be used with any SharePoint list. Just do what it says to do:

1. Make a list called SimpleApp on a SharePoint Online site.
2. Put items for **Vanilla, Chocolate, and Strawberry** in a section called **Title**.

Even if you make a list with a lot of different sections, like text, times, numbers, and currency, the steps for making an app will still work the same way. Keep in mind that Power Apps does not work with all SharePoint data types.

Create an app from within Power Apps

1. Log in to Power Apps.
2. From the home screen, choose one of the following options based on how you want to make your app:
- To make a dynamic photo app with a single page, pick one of these options:
  - **Start with data > Select external data > From SharePoint.**

- o **Start with a page design > Gallery connected to external data > From SharePoint**.
- **Choose Start with an app design > From SharePoint** to make a three-screen mobile app.

3. You will be asked to make a SharePoint link if you don't already have one. To change the link, click on the "**...**" button. This will let you switch accounts or make a new connection.

4. Type in the URL for SharePoint and then click Connect. Choose a new site instead.

5. Pick a list, then click "**Create app**." Your app will open in PowerApps Studio, where you can plan, build, and oversee it. Before you use this app or give it to other people, you may want to make some more changes. Before moving on, it's a good idea to save your work by clicking the "Save" icon in the top right spot. Name your app, then click "**Save**."

Create an app from within SharePoint Online

From the SharePoint Online taskbar, you can make an app of a list. The app will show up as a view of the list. The app can be used on a computer browser as well as an iOS or Android device.

1. Open a list in SharePoint Online. Then, go to **Integrate > Power Apps > Create an app**.

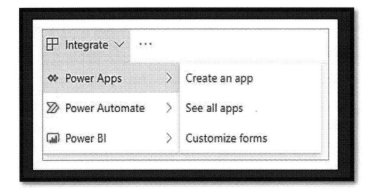

2. Type a name for your app in the text box that comes up, and then click Create.
- Your computer browser will open a new tab that shows the app you made from your list. You can change the app in Power Apps Studio, where it shows up.

3. (**Optional**) First, refresh the browser tab for your list by clicking on it and then hitting F5. Next, do these things to run or control your app:
- Click **Open** to run the app in a new browser tab.
- Choose "**Make this view public**" to let other people in your company use the app.

Let other people change your app by sharing it with Can change permissions.
- Click **Remove this view** to get rid of the view in SharePoint.

Delete the app to get rid of it from Power Apps.

Note: At the moment, apps made from the list don't show up in Power Apps Mobile.

Use Sharepoint or SQL on-premises

These steps should be taken if you want to make an app that uses an external on-premises data source like SharePoint or SQL on-premises.

1. Log in to Power Apps.
2. Click on **Create** in the menu on the left.
3. Choose **SharePoint or SQL** based on the type of data source you're linking to.
4. Click on "**New connection**," then pick "**SharePoint** or **SQL**."
5. Click on Connect using on-premises data connection, fill in the necessary details, and then click on **Create**.
- Once your link is ready, click on it to see a list of tables that can be used with the connection.
6. Pick a table, and then click **Connect**.

FAQs (frequently asked questions)

What is the difference between SharePoint Online and SharePoint On-Premises?

While SharePoint On-Premises is installed and managed on an organization's computers, SharePoint Online is the cloud-based version of SharePoint that is housed on Microsoft 365. On-Premises gives you more control over the system, while SharePoint Online lets you add more users, get regular changes, and view the site from anywhere.

Who can use SharePoint Online?

It can be used by anyone who has a Microsoft 365 plan that includes SharePoint Online. People from outside your company, like partners or buyers, can also visit your SharePoint Online sites if you have permission to do so.

What Internet browsers are supported for using SharePoint Online?

The following browsers can all be used to get to SharePoint Online: Apple Safari, Google Chrome, Internet Explorer, or Microsoft Edge. However, some functions might not work right in older browsers or browsers that aren't enabled.

How do I log into my SharePoint Online site?

You need a Microsoft 365 account and a good username and password to get into your SharePoint Online site. You can use the straight URL of your SharePoint Online site, if you know it, or go to the [SharePoint homepage] and sign in with your passwords there.

How can I easily find and access SharePoint Online sites that I have been given access to?

The SharePoint app launcher can help you find and get to SharePoint Online sites that you are allowed to see. You can get to it by clicking on the app launcher button in the site's top left corner. From that page, you can see the sites you just viewed, followed, or made. You can use the name or URL of a site to find it too.

How do I view all site content on a SharePoint Online site?

You can view all site material on a SharePoint Online site by clicking the Settings button in the top-right area and then selecting Site Contents. This is what will show you all of your site's lists, books, pages, and apps. This page is also where you can add, change, or remove site information.

How can I create a new site in SharePoint?

You can make a new SharePoint site by going to the home page, clicking on "Create site," and picking the right site design. Team Site, Communication Site, and Document Center are all common site designs.

What is a SharePoint list?

Like a worksheet, a SharePoint list is a collection of data set up in rows and sections. You can use lists to keep track of things, organize your work, and store information like contacts, events, or supplies.

How can I customize SharePoint sites?

Features like web parts, styles, and page layouts can be used to make SharePoint sites unique. For more complicated customizations, like processes and custom apps, you can also use the Microsoft Power Platform or SharePoint Designer tools.

What is SharePoint workflow?

By setting up a list of jobs and actions that need to be done based on certain conditions, SharePoint workflows simplify and improve business processes. You can use SharePoint Designer, Power Automate, or other workflow tools to make workflows.

How does versioning work in SharePoint?

Users can track changes over time using SharePoint's versioning feature for papers and list items. Users can view, go back to, or compare different versions of a document using versioning, which aids in document control and collaboration.

What is the purpose of content types in SharePoint?

In SharePoint, content types set up how information, actions, and document styles are organized and defined. They make it possible to organize and handle material across sites, libraries, and lists in the same way.

How can I integrate SharePoint with Microsoft Teams?

The collaboration tool Microsoft Teams works well with SharePoint. A smooth collaboration experience is provided by the fact that Teams users can view and share SharePoint documents right from the Teams interface.

What is the role of SharePoint in document management?

Versioning, check-in/check-out, information, and document processes are just a few of the strong document management tools that SharePoint has to offer. It makes it easier for groups to store, organize, and work together on paper.

How can I ensure security in SharePoint?

Access control lists (ACLs), user permissions, and role-based security are just a few of the strong security tools that come with SharePoint. Multi-factor authentication (MFA) and data loss prevention (DLP) rules can also be used by businesses to make security better.

Can SharePoint be accessed on mobile devices?

Yes, SharePoint is mobile-friendly, and users can use mobile apps to view SharePoint sites and information. On top of that, there are SharePoint mobile apps for both iOS and Android devices.

How do I share files and folders on SharePoint Online?

On SharePoint Online, you can share folders and files with people inside and outside your company. You need at least change permission on a file or folder before you can share it. You can pick a file or folder and click the share button on the menu bar, or you can click the share button next to it. After that, you can select the people you want to share with or copy a link that you can send to anyone. You can also pick the level of access you want to give, like "view only," "edit," or "specific people1."

How do I create a team site on SharePoint Online?

A team site is a type of SharePoint site that lets you work on projects, papers, and tasks with other people on your team. You need a Microsoft 365 group or a Microsoft Teams team to make a team site in SharePoint Online. You can click the **"Create Site"** button on the SharePoint home page or go to the site settings of a group or team that already exists to make a team site. Then you can pick a name for the site, a statement, and a private setting. You can change the look of your site by adding pages, web parts, and apps.

How do I sync SharePoint Online files to my computer?

With the OneDrive sync app, you can move files from SharePoint Online to your computer. You can then view your files when you're not online and keep them up to date on all of your devices. You need the OneDrive sync app and to be signed in with your Microsoft 365 accounts to sync files from SharePoint Online to your computer. You can sync files in SharePoint Online by hitting the **"Sync"** button on the command bar next to the library or folder you want to sync. This is where you can pick where to put your sync folder and change its settings. You can also use the OneDrive sync app to change your sync settings and preferences.

Conclusion

This SharePoint guidance is like an easy-to-use map that will help you understand and get the most out of Microsoft's collaboration tool. We've talked about a lot, from what SharePoint is and how it can help you manage papers and work on projects with other people. We looked at how you can change SharePoint to fit your needs, make sites for different reasons, and even set it up to do things automatically to save time. A part also talks about combining SharePoint Online with the version you run on your computers, with the main goal of making sure everything works well. The "Frequently Asked Questions" section is like a quick guide sheet because it answers the most common questions people have about SharePoint. You might find these answers useful whether you are new to SharePoint or have been using it for a while. For the most part, this guidance will help you understand SharePoint and show you how to use it well and get the most out of its features. The information here can help you get the most out of Microsoft's SharePoint, no matter how much experience you have or how new you are to it.

INDEX

G

H

J

N

O

T

Printed in Great Britain
by Amazon

6ab23cbb-9ea5-4b2a-b0e8-2dd02c7a2d4fR01